UNALOME

The journey towards Authentic self

Shweta Bharti

Sakāl Publications

UNALOME

Sakal Media Pvt. Ltd.
595, Budhwar Peth,
Pune – 411002, India

www.sakalpublications.com
sakalprakashan@esakal.com

The views expressed in this book are those of the Authors and do not necessarily reflect the views of the Editors and the Publishers.

Although the Editors and the Authors have made every effort to ensure that the information in this book is correct at the time of printing, the Editors, Authors and the Publishers do not assume and hereby disclaim any liability to any party for any loss, damage, or disruption caused by errors or omissions, whether such errors or omissions result from negligence, accident, or any other cause.

ISBN No.: 978-81-19311-60-6

Edited by: Yogita Vaidya

Cover Design: Mitali Panganti

Typesetting: MAP Systems, Bengaluru

Printed in India by Sakal Media Pvt. Ltd.

In the loving memory of my mother,
Mrs. Kiran K Giri

And my mother-in-law,
Mrs Sushila M Bharti

Contents

FOREWORD

If there was one book on how self-awareness can help you achieve completeness in life in modern times, that would be "Unalome" by Dr. Shweta Bharti. Right from the first page, this book could connect with me at a deeper level. It is an honest and sincere attempt by Dr. Shweta to translate her experience into a literary piece.

In today's world, people are struggling to keep up to the demands of a fast-paced life. Our career aspirations have sky-rocketed, and we gear ourselves up to fulfill them without paying attention to our true self.Some of us actually reach the peak, only to realize the void within. We call it an information age, but we cannot be farther away from knowing who we are, and what we want.The natural human emotions such as fear, anxiety, sadness have now metamorphosed into diseases such as hypertension, nervous breakdown, cardiac problems, and more, because we keep living with these emotions for a prolonged period of time.

When we are so focused on the achievements in the outer world, why do we feel so empty inside?

Unalome is a "no nonsense" book that serves as a guide to help you understand your unique self, your true nature and grow as an individual who you were meant to be. It will help you in your journey towards self-realization. Unalome stays away from any unrealistic expectations, and emphasizes on being your authentic self.

This book is written in a simple language for everyone to understand. While reading Unalome, I remembered the famous scene from the movie "The Matrix" where Morpheus asks Neo about which pill would the latter like to take, the blue pill which will take Neo back to the illusive world, or the red pill which will show Neo what the real world is – dark. Neo chooses the red pill, and that's how he starts his journey into the real world and eventually transforms it into a bright, happy and authentic world that it's meant to be. This book is the red pill, and you are Neo.

Manish Mohan Grampurohit
Founder, Corporhythm (a strategic brand building firm)
Writer, Poet, Artist
Ex-Information Technologist

From the Author's Desk

I believe searching for yourself is often a misinterpreted concept. It is more about remembering the true nature of yourself. Having found one's true nature makes everyone happy, joyous, and blissful, with a sense of peace within. If whatever you are doing today does not bring you this sense of self, it means there is a need for some change in your working pattern. There is something that is making you stressful: be it your relationships, your work, your circumstances. Yet, none of this may be under your control. What you can control, however, is yourself, what you can change is yourself. These changes can be minute or drastic, but unless you make them to create a life that is more fulfilling you will always have a sense of inadequacy and incompleteness.

What corresponds to the journey of finding yourself is finding your natural sense of being. Finding the joy, which is not outside but within yourself. Finding this state, and maintaining it will enrich your life. For life is not meant to live in agony, in sadness. It is meant to feel a sense of bliss.

It will not come by blindly following a path that others might show you but listening to your inner voice closely, patiently, and compassionately. Following it bit by bit, slowly but steadily and then becoming the light and showing a path to others, to those who really need it.

Life is not just about your career, it is not just about your relationships, and not just for material gain. It is also about expanding your spirit: to grow, to cherish, to flourish.

Life is to live, laugh, and love.

Life is to lift yourself up, to solve the mystery, make it simple. It is like a simplified solution of mathematics. And that can only happen if we know the formula. It is about knowing yourself – your strengths and weaknesses, your values, your definition to everything you come across. It is reorganising what is not working and escalating what is working. It is clearing out the debris of age-old beliefs, and your mind of unwanted thoughts, making space for a new, fresh, fragrant breeze that is soulful to enter. It is about meeting life with a fresh perspective and creating that perspective for yourself on your own by following your passions.

It is also about giving up to what is not you, what makes you feel unwanted. Keeping strong boundaries ensures such things do not fall in your path. It is breaking the glass ceiling that is holding you back from progress. Letting go of negative patterns that are no longer welcome while at the same time being compassionate and kind. It is about showing gratitude for all that you have, to all those who gave your life some depth and height.

It is about living life your way. In a way that gives you a feeling of rapture, that makes you realise how splendid the colours of life are. It's just a matter of how you use them to make a masterpiece of your life.

Unalome is about the awakening of your spirit, searching for your original happy, blissful being, attaining a sense of peace and maintaining it. It is about discovering the purpose and meaning of life and ultimately realising the truth of life, living life in a way that is more fulfilling according to your own perceptions. It is about healing yourself, your old unhealed wounds, rearranging your beliefs and discovering that everyone has a unique way of attaining mental peace. The truth is that this path towards remembering your own joyful true self or your authentic self that is not deterred by outward issues and burdens takes time, takes courage.

What I refer to here as healing is grounding yourself to create emotional and mental stability, while attaining and maintaining a peaceful state of mind.

Although this is not a guidebook for doing anything in a particular way, it is a catalyst to start the thinking process in every "YOU" who is reading it to find your own True Authentic Blissful Balanced self who is ready to take UP challenges of life with positive attitude and passing with flying colours in this test called LIFE.

There comes a time when you stop:
    Proving yourself
    Explaining yourself
    Hiding yourself.
    Behind all that
    That's untrue
    That's unworthy
    That's a veil.
    That That's
    Not you.

You stop showing up
    For all that
    Makes you pressurised

Overwhelmed
Triggered
Annoyed
Unfulfilled.

That is the time when you show up
    For yourself
    To find a you
    Who is pure
    Who is truthful
    Who is still
    Yet growing
    To the fullest.
    You that
    You were
    Meant to be
    To fulfil the purpose
    Of your being.

Introduction

Is it easy to leave everything? Is it easy not to feel anything except sorrow and grief?

I have always run from sorrow. I don't like to be sad with that heavy weight on my chest, with that lump in my throat, with tears in my eyes, and those headaches. It's laborious to digest grief. In each such arduous situation, I invariably keep myself occupied in order to forget about the situation, the difficulty. Little did I realise that it does not free you from sadness, from sorrow, from grief. Rather, it keeps on building those feelings of unworthiness, incompleteness, insecurity, and fear of facing similar situations again. It does not make you strong but hesitant; powerless to the declination so much that moving back to the original joyous state of mind seems like a task. Besides, you accumulate those unhealthy emotions for everyone involved in the situation. It disturbs your overall harmony. While you cannot control what others feel for you, you can have complete control over what you feel.

In order to gain that control you need to heal yourself. Heal to the core. Your unspoken wounds, your untold traumas that are repressed within you for years, they have now engraved in your memories, your system. And each time there is a similar trigger, they show their faces with more intensity. They become memories of unpleasantness, unwantedness. You keep these memories inside of you in a dormant state. And when similar scenarios perpetuate, which in due course of time will occur without fail as it is the way nature tests you, again the cycle begins. It continues over and over in a loop.

Until…

You HEAL, you ACCEPT, you FEEL EVERY PAIN you are subjected to. It is the unhealed part of yourself that attracts similar situations in your life. It is 'Like Attracts Like'.

This does not mean that you are wrong or the people you are dealing with are. If you assess your group, you always could befriend people who could align with you, your thoughts. Similarly, you perpetually come across people who have similar past life experiences or traumas like you. After an initial good relationship – be it of any kind – there is tussle, hustle, rift, and friction for the smallest of reasons. As a result, people whom you thought were just like you go away from you. You find yourself rejected, alone, unhappy, angry, unfulfilled just like the previous time. You weren't expecting this after the last unpleasant experience of yours. You had thought you were alright, that you are light and not carrying the heavy burden of the past any longer. Yet you are in distress. 'Oh no! Why? Why this? Why is this happening again? Why me again?' the child inside you cries, demands for regard. Nevertheless, the stubborn adult you who believes in the practicality of life, who has various responsibilities and jobs feels: 'This is a superfluous mess. I am not a child anymore. I am a resolute human being. Meagre situations like these, frugal people like these do not deserve me. They have no position to deal with me. I am all good. Only thing that I need to do is move on.' The mind creates an easy trap of distraction from pain that arises from an embroilment that you just went through:

'can I invest my time in doing things, can I go to an old place I like. Let's go shopping, drink, go on a vacation, be with people, eat junk, and dance.'

Another reaction could be putting the other person on a pedestal and of wanting to forgive them by thinking: 'I am the problem, it is my fault that I am at this locus today.'

Which one is wise? Neither!

The first one leads to resentment, a sense of pride, of passing judgement over another person, demeaning another person, cultivating a sense of ascendancy within. The second one, meanwhile, advances one to having immense low self-worth, devaluation. It pushes them from the edge of an avalanche.

Presuppose that there is a kind of trauma that everyone undergoes in one's lifetime. Is it healthy when we consider this scenario in the panorama of a community where each one dwells with variegated kinds of insults? Is it healthy to have such individuals in society? If we count society as a whole, having almost every individual being traumatised at least once in their lifetime, intentionally or unintentionally by ordeal, how will that community be?

Therefore, it is not surprising when we open the newspaper or watch the news to stumble upon incidences of violence, murder, theft, war, rape, domestic violence and suchlike. It is ubiquitous in recent times to comment on climate change. Natural calamities, new diseases, changes in atmosphere, global warming. Are these all skimpy co-occurrences?

Diverse elements in nature are all interrelated; they have influence on each other. It is the moon that leads to high and low tides on earth. It is sunlight that helps facilitate, nurture, and sustain life on earth. And what is that? Energy! A form of energy giving rise to another form of energy. It's a modification of energy from one form into the other.

When energy that is coming from millions and trillions of miles away can lead to such drastic results, can we envisage how human beings as a collective would be exerting energy in this atmosphere, on earth's energy field? And when most of us are deeply distorted in our vehemence, which in turn distorts our energy field, our aura, how much do you think we are distorting the atmosphere around in a fatalistic way? Therefore, let's not solely blame our actions, it's our distorted energy field furthermore contributing to the pernicious transpose.

Is there any solution to this?

The solution is healing. Healing of the human race as a collective. And what I and you can do for it: I heal myself and you heal yourself.

Interestingly, you cannot simply start this healing journey because someone has told you to do so, unless you have the desire to do so from within. Understanding that there is something that needs to be paid attention to is the first step of self-realisation.

*

When we are born, we are in our purest form, in the natural sense of being – fearless, joyful, happy, yet observant, learning, adapting, accepting. Through this observation and adaptation, as we grow up, we get conditioned by our immediate family members and the society at large. We adapt to belief patterns that at times do not resonate with who we are. The foremost issue every individual deals with is pessimistic archetypes where they are unconsciously schooled to underrate themselves. It can be through their physical appearance, caste, creed, community, nationality, intelligence…

the list is endless. This pessimistic conditioning – that one needs to follow to match the mandate of society – tames the natural spirit of that being. This creates disruption in the minds of the individuals which, when spread over a long period of time, the person either becomes subservient to it, devising a weaker personality, or the becomes a rebel creating revolution.

Even though the conditioning system, as a whole, cannot be labelled as invalid, yet when it is not in harmony with an individual's own value system or their own nature, the discrepancy becomes a fuel in the disruption of the life path. Blindly believing what anyone tells you, without questioning it, without knowing its significance or futility, without using your own wisdom is another way of self-sabotage.

Every individual is a perfect being with some qualities that are more dominant over others. Honouring those qualities of an individual can be a substantial stimulus for further growth of an individual. However, this scarcely happens. And if this does not happen externally, then recognising those qualities yourself and bringing them forth – the qualities that gives an individual the joy of living a fulfilled life – is obligatory. But this is easier said than done. Identifying your own qualities, nurturing them and gaining prowess, is no cakewalk.

Individuals have to follow the rules of society to fit in, which often crush their own impulses. This becomes burdensome at a certain stage which leads to inner turmoil. Then the question arises: despite doing everything that's been told, why is it grinding to attain, to maintain a joyous state? Why is there a perception of incompleteness? And when you realise that your ability to sustain such a way of life is over, you are unable to do it anymore, and you feel the need to explore the qualities within yourself, ignite that fire within. And here begins your journey to the unknown, the journey of finding yourself.

They would dictate you do this, do that:
    "Oh how can you say that, you are so wrong".
    They would want you to follow meaningless rules
    And then would tell you how to be a slave of those rules.
    They would tell you how you are not any good
    In whatever you do.
    They would embark if you don't listen to them your life is
    totally screwed.
    They perfectly take care to change you into what you are not
    From all those natural instincts that you had got.
    Then one day you realise that I have done everything that
    I had been told.
    Still what is the matter, life feels so dull.
    Then that is the day… the day you have woken up
    From years of that torment, that slumber.
    A time has come to break the pattern
    Of age-old beliefs and of being someone else
    And to find who you are and why you are there.
    The path will be painful, full of difficulties.
    You will feel lonely, as if nothing is left.
    Still go on... on the way you are guided.
    There will be the divine who will help you
    And those who accept you as your true self.

You might feel on the way you have lost a lot
    But then you will realise that it's you who matters at last.
    And there will be a day when you find the lost self

After shedding all those layers that society had trapped
you in.
From that day a beautiful butterfly will emerge from
the cocoon.

Security

What is Security?

As children we feel secure when we are with familiar people, in a familiar environment. When we can feel the warmth, we are at ease.

When we feel insecure as a child or even as an adult, we get a sense of something that is being snatched away from us. When we feel insulted, ridiculed, rejected, abandoned, or any other situation which is not in alignment with what we actually perceive ourselves as. For example, when you are asked to go to a very boisterous place, but you find being in quiet places more comfortable or vice versa.

When we see a child, he or she is always happy, living in the present moment, whenever they are feeling secure. When their sense of security is at stake, there is transgression by children in the form of tantrums, crying, and aggression.

In adults, the sense of security is in the form of basic needs, comfort zone, financial stability, prestige, fame, relationships. There are numerous factors. And more so, they are divergent for each individual. No matter the age, there is a tender, fragile part of ourselves that tends to preserve our innocence, our zest towards life. Owing to the naivete of this innocence, it exhilarates with joy in the smallest of pleasures and sobs in situations that are undesirable. Insecurity of any kind makes this part of ours feel insecure. This part of ours is the child that we carry within ourselves. The inner child! It is this inner child that creates shadows within one's personalities based on previous undesirable situations, by labels given to us by society.

When there is loss of security, this inner child, that we consider is all grown up, demands this security back. It shows up in the form of emotional instability and the shadow-self shows up as well. The shadow-self is full of doubts and negative beliefs. It pulls you down the moment you try to get up. It tells you about your unworthiness, reminds you of your weakness.

When it comes to healing, you have to heal your inner child and all the shadows that you have gathered due to unhealthy situations. It takes courage to accept that you have these shadows, as you don't know what shadows you might have, how much time it might take to heal them, what the process might be, and what the eventual outcome will be.

But beyond all this, after you heal yourself, there is a door to bliss that is waiting for you. Yes, it is there, not very far from you. All you need to do is start… The key that opens the Door to Bliss is in our hands. We merely need to make a decision and then act.

How to Deal with Insecurity Arising from Unwanted Situations?

There is a stigma in society towards expressing what you actually feel, especially when you are not in the best of your mental status. Just as the physical form of our body requires care from time to time, the mental and emotional form of our body also needs attention, care, and nourishment. Having a 'strong mind' is an overrated concept wherein everyone is told that being vulnerable is akin to a crime. This is the reason why it takes a lot of time to accept that there is a problem.

Another barrier, which is a reason why many people do not pay attention to their mental state, is time constraint. Life has become a race where everyone is running behind material success. Everyone is busy doing hard work to attain goals, fulfil social standards, meet responsibilities, and survive. Nevertheless, goals that are attained at the price of one's mental health are a bit too expensive. Undesirable situations do occur all the time in everyone's life. The third reason for not accepting the hitch is actually the fear of getting triggered again based on past experiences.

Unless we courageously decide to face our mental trauma and deal with it ourselves, we are open to becoming vulnerable again. We test our own bravery while we cannot attain the sense of security within.

This lack of security results in anxiety. This anxiety presents in the form of physical symptoms: palpitations, sweats, thirst, eating disorders, sleep disorders, and in chronic cases, even diseases at the cognitive level of being unable to take decisions, to focus, to take a stand for oneself. This anxiety comes in a loop. The more you get anxious the more situations arise that bring anxiety, and thus it becomes a vicious cycle.

How to Break this Loop of Anxiety?

The only way to deal with the anxiety that emerges when we land up in an undesirable situation is by accepting what we feel. Acknowledge it. 'Feeling' the feeling is essential. Staying with that feeling without being hard on yourself, without judging yourself or others is necessary.

Unless you are in that unpleasant feeling, your inner child will not feel heard. Hearing gives a sense of assurance, a sense of courtesy. When heard, this inner child lets itself free and tells you about the trouble it has faced. At times, from childhood: the memories when it felt unworthy, bitter, angry, sad. The pain it perceived during those situations. Whatever comes out at that moment is okay! It gradually lessens the pain, the unpleasant feeling.

At times, the pain might be so much that you may not be able to handle it all by yourself. Whenever it becomes overwhelming, speaking out to someone whom you trust: a family member, a friend, a therapist, a mentor can be of help. Just the feeling of being heard can make you feel lighter. While it is one of the more immediate ways of feeling better, it's not a permanent solution. Being heard makes your inner child feel secure for some time but at the same time, resolving the issues completely is a prime requisite.

Positive Attitude

Positive attitude is a buzz. Pessimism is prohibited. Everyone tries to go in accordance with the mindset to be positive, happy, and optimistic. Yet when there's a trigger in our outer reality, it disturbs our balance and throws us off into the depths of negativities again. Bouncing back to a positive attitude can sometimes prove as a backbreaker.

The positive mindset aka positive attitude is a function of the frontal cortex of the brain, which helps us make rational decisions and work in accordance with situations by thinking wisely, in situations that are considered normal/non-threatening by the human brain. Whenever there is a trigger in the outer reality, this rational frontal cortex shuts itself down and the sympathetic system takes over, which has a basic survival instinct of flight or fight. Run away or face the situation. And this reflex works upon previous experiences and conditioning from society.

Inherent beliefs that have been instilled over the course of your life in your mind of being insufficient, of not being worthy enough, overpower the positive attitude, diminishing its results in comparison to the efforts put in, which all the more hits harder. To overcome this barrier in the subconscious mind, it is recommended to affirm yourself everyday with mantras such as:

- I am happy!
- I am powerful!

- I am abundant!
- I am healthy!

In spite of this, deep down in our subconscious, a voice often says, 'You know this is not your truth, right?'

Ever wondered where this voice comes from? It comes from your unhealed self. The tender, innocent child self of yours who existed at some point, which you may not even recollect now as someone significant but was told, was made to believe the exact opposite of how things were.

Affirmations that you are supposed to chant every day no longer work after a certain initial period of good results. One may obtain short term success in the form of financial gain or the accomplishment of a goal. Nonetheless, after this short span of success that one attains in a few areas of life, one's unhealed trauma reflects itself in other areas where you might still feel lacking, unfulfilled. For example, someone is earning a good amount of money but has troubled relationships. Someone who has very good relationships but has fiscal issues. If everything's fine, health can be an issue. There are a number of scenarios where our unhealed-self lurks unwantedly in our lives without our own realisation.

Have you lately asked yourself:

- How am I feeling?
- Am I Happy?
- Have you closed your eyes & felt a sense of peace? Of not having been overblown by day-to-day activities?
- Have you felt secure?

Acceptance

What we resist persists.

The incidents happening around us and the reactions and circumstances arising out of it are not in our control. Therefore, it is important to understand that we cannot change something that is out of our control, what we can change, however, is our response towards it. And we can do it only when we completely accept the happenings that are occurring around us and we do not let them deter our own mental well-being.

Acceptance is a different process for every individual. But it isn't an easy one for sure. For a while it may feel that you have accepted a particular situation outwardly, yet deep down you still carry hurt and resentment, and anger might still be stagnant within you. Surpassing the trauma of these negative emotions takes time and is actually different for each person.

In this situation, the first step is to calm yourself and stop overthinking. Meditation can help in a great way. Meditation is about accessing the stillness and depth within your mind by negating constant thought processes. It is a deep state of awareness that increases a sense of tranquillity. Guided meditation for a certain time in a day is a vital step that can be followed easily. Initially, it can be difficult to sit quietly in one place with an equally still mind but you can start with a few minutes at first. At a point you will realise that depending on your consistency, with each passing day, the duration of stillness, thoughtless state increases.

The purpose of meditation is not to focus or become thoughtless but to observe the thoughts that come to your mind as a third person, without being judgemental about yourself. To look at these thoughts without making judgments. As days pass, the thoughts will be less, less and less. Though there will suddenly be a re-appearance of thoughts, specifically when unwanted hassles happen in the outer reality, the gist here is to not get disheartened but to continue with the process of meditation.

In order to overcome the incessant creation of thoughts within, you can take the help of your breath. Observing your breath diverts the attention of your overactive mind from its constant thoughts and lets it focus on breathing. For the mind is ever observant, it likes to observe the things that are dynamic. Breath is the vital force of life, which continues without a break since we are born. One that we often take for granted, even though it connects our inner world with the expansive universe of which we are an integral part. Observe that gift of creation, which is priceless. Feel its coming in and going out. The movement of your chest with each inhalation and exhalation. Be present while breathing. Observe until which part of your body the breath goes in and how it goes out, the flaring of nostrils while breathing, what is the temperature of the air coming in, warm or cold. Observe everything that you can.

Do you feel any sensation on any part of the body: head, chest, hands, legs, forehead? Observe the sensation while it is there without asking why I am feeling so. Do you see colours in front of your closed eyes? Are they still or moving? In which direction are they moving?

Without your realisation, you will be in a zone of stillness, calmness, where there is nothing but quiescence. A quiescence that is so relaxing, yet it would be impossible to guess when you have entered it but it's only when you are about to come out of it that you become aware of it. You will feel a deep sense of trance, complete stoppage of thoughts. As it happens, you will not be able to recollect the time for which you were there in that phase. It can extend from seconds to minutes to hours. One may lose their sense of body in this phase. The body becomes so light that it is almost non-existent. Stimuli for coming out of this stage are often loud sounds or heaviness or numbness in any part of the body or a sudden eureka over a situation or the answer to a question.

An experience of this trance-like stage is revitalising. The more you practise, the more you improve your focus; your mood swings decrease, and your potential to deal with tough, complex situations increases. Your confidence reaches new heights as your mind perceives it as a victory over negative emotions. It is a positive effort taken by you for yourself. You might even notice yourself smiling in the mirror, feeling good about yourself. Negative thoughts will reduce, but not disappear though. However, their frequency decreases along with the time required to transform negative thought patterns into positive ones.

This space of negative thoughts is replaced by thoughts that are positive or neutral. Meditation helps you with the profound realisation of your own traits, your own behaviour. As you become more stable and balanced, you are able to identify at what point of time you are losing your balance, when you are feeling anger, and what are the things that trigger you. You change from having distorted behaviour to a balanced one sooner, compared to your previous self, before you started practising meditation.

It is crucial here to acknowledge that you don't immediately lose all your negative traits with meditation, but it's your perspective towards it that changes, which leads to different approaches in similar circumstances which happen to be more balanced. Your response is more neutral. You tend to shift from negative to positive more swiftly.

Your reaction towards others becomes more compassionate, as your understanding of a situation improves. As you come closer to your own self, you stop pleasing other people merely to keep in touch with them. You become more comfortable in your own skin. You do not indulge in drama of any kind anymore. You become composed. You smile more. You feel more love towards people. There is a certain state of joy and peace that resides within you. Forgiving comes without constraint. Your awareness of others' emotions, energies enhances. You strive to apprehend the reasoning behind the behaviours of others. You do not judge other people, and thus, you do not judge yourself!

Mindfulness

Mindfulness is being in complete awareness of what you are doing. In our routine life, we do things for the sake of doing them. We finish up chores with a hundred other thoughts in our mind. Naturally, we do not get the desired output, nor do we enjoy the task at hand. Mindfulness is when we effortlessly learn to focus all our complete, undivided attention towards what we are doing. When we do anything with complete focus, we enjoy the process more. At the same time, we get rid of all the distractions and our ever-restless mind takes pause. Quieting the mind is necessary in order to attain a state of peace for it is our hyperactive mind which creates a false sense of disharmony in our lives, which creates an illusion of pitiful things being perceived as big problems and creates a false sense of fear by unnecessarily magnifying them even more. Therefore, we need to put this mind to rest from unnecessary overthinking, reasoning, and guessing. When the mind is at rest, we attain a natural sense of being.

When we engage our minds in certain physical activities such as exercise, and games, it focuses itself into that activity. Our body needs exercise in order to keep ourselves healthy. At the same time, it causes the brain to release 'feel good' chemicals like endorphins and serotonin. It also helps break the loop of negative thought patterns.

Just as we exercise our body, we can also exercise our breath with breathing exercises. When you breathe slowly, focusing on the in & out movement of air, it calms your mind, gives a break to incessant thoughts, and reduces heart rate. Simple breathing exercises such as Pranayama not only help to keep our lungs healthy but also to keep our thoughts more towards the positive side.

Another way to engage a hyperactive mind is doing what you have a passion for. It can be anything that you like – music, dance, arts, working on your creative side on something that you had a passion for but stopped doing over time due to other responsibilities. You can start by doing it for a brief period, as and when required, when your heart calls you to do it. When you adopt a new hobby that excites you, it works in many ways to reduce stress. You learn a new skill, you focus your attention into it, which leads to a sense of engagement, and you create something new out of it that gives you a sense of accomplishment. Not only that, it also boosts your self-esteem manifold.

Working on different aspects to improve one's emotional stability surely makes one a better, understanding, peaceful, and compassionate human being. When you work on yourself, your heart fills with gratitude and radiates joy. It starts healing every day, more and more!

If You Heal and Become A Better Version of Yourself, Then Does This Stop People from Misunderstanding You?

The main reason that we create chaos in our mind pertaining to any stressful situation is we live our lives based on people's opinion, whilst knowing that is a thing that we can never have control upon. Even when you are on your healing journey people will misunderstand you, misinterpret you.

Yet along your healing journey, you will get connected with people who are more alike – the ones who appreciate you, like you for who you are. People who do not have good feelings about you may gradually start drifting away, unless they themselves try to be more aware of the goodness of life. Rest of the people simply fall away altogether because you are no longer the person whom they knew. You have changed yourself, refined yourself and they do not identify with this refined version. They will find it strange, at times even be jealous of you because they once considered you like them and now they are unable to understand the progress you have made in this brief time. It is not that you have changed for the worse but it's their perception, the prejudice that they hold about you that shatters, and they are unable to handle this.

This phase of people drifting away from you can possibly bring a sense of anxiety, an unease of being on your own. Though, it is not as such. When you focus on yourself, your natural state of being, you are supported by none other than the universe. This phase is to understand yourself in a more profound way. When you start doing it, new doors will open for you. People get attracted towards you – you who are now revised, refined, renewed.

You are more appreciated for what you are than what you used to pretend to be. You become more open, more accepting towards people and situations. This occurs because you have harmonised yourself to the vibrations of your authentic self, of how you actually are, underneath all the adapted layers. This vibration of the highest power of your authentic self produces a frequency of resonance, reduces resistance, and gradually enables you to walk towards accomplishing what you were meant to.

In this process, you often help people with their botheration as well. If not in a direct manner, then indirectly by inspiring them to follow their heart, to go closer to their true self.

Identity Crisis

Identity crisis is a phase that comes in every healing journey. When we heal, we find ourselves becoming different from what we used to be. As we become more open, joyous, accepting, we create healthy boundaries with people. We hold a certain level of self-esteem and do not fall prey to manipulation as we used to before. This creates a certain change in perception of ourselves in our minds, leading to an identity crisis.

Why so? Because it brings about the death of the ego-based you – who you used to be, who you were perceived to be, that weak you, that subservient you, that you who was conditioned to be a certain way, is now changed to 'someone' who is striking, trustworthy, and significant. One who is able to shift their thinking, the paradigms, who confronts their boundaries, who does not relate to traditions that no longer serve them, someone who believes in being conscious in the true sense of the word. Therefore, this change is not undesirable. It is a remarkable switch that makes you better than your previous ordinary self. This is the process of transformation – the transformation of a caterpillar into a beautiful butterfly with colourful wings who knows how to fly without any heavy burdens, where life finally becomes sheer joy.

When We Say We Transform Like A Butterfly, Will The Transformation Process Be Painful?

Healing is the journey of awakening your spirit. There is a myriad of incertitude and chaos, which often is not easy to deal with. This can lead to completely different actions, that can be the polar opposite from your usual demeanour. Your dressing style might change – if you were more modern before, you may adapt to a traditional dressing sense and if traditional before you may become more modern. If you were not expressive before you start expressing yourself more effortlessly whereas if you were talkative before you could become calmer. There is a certain pull to try things that you never did before. You act in a way that could be far from what you thought you were. It creates confusion in the minds of yours and of the people who knew you before. Even your habits, eating patterns, sleep patterns may alter. Diminished hunger and sleeplessness is common when you explore yourself. There can be frequent episodes of inconsolable cries. You might wake up in the middle of the night and start crying out of nowhere in a way that you never cried before. There can be pain in your chest and throat, a sense of hollowness, and disconnection. You feel anxious. Activities that charmed you before do not remain as gripping. You yearn towards the unknown. There can be a sudden splurge of artistic qualities in you for they help you attain a calm state of mind, to stop the chaos going on in your mind. You start questioning belief systems, and all the people around you. You realise nothing is permanent. Everything, every relation is there, just for the time being. There is nothing like forever, as change is the only entity that is constant. If you lose anything or anyone, it is not because you lack or they do, but simply because your karma with them has ended. If someone new enters your life, it is by the cause that you have certain karma with them now. There are episodes of sudden realisations. It is as if a glitzy, shimmery curtain has been taken off of your eyes and you, unanticipatedly, are finally seeing the harsh reality.

In spite of the daily juggles of life, you learn to listen to the sound of silence. You admire the beauty of nature. Being in nature calms you, you realise the magnificence of nature, the divine, the beauty that you had forsaken priorly in your chores.

The reality is that we all are on our own. The truth is that everyone holds different truths for themselves. Though we are dependent on each other, being overly reliant on anyone more than one's own self is codependency and that is not healthy for you or for your soul's growth. Since, codependency is a toxic trait and is not apt for your growth or of anyone else's, you need to find and attain a state of interdependency.

What Will This Transformation Process Help with and Why Is It Important?

This process aids you in finding your authentic self on your own, as you access the depths of your subconscious. It is like searching within your own soul. Remembering your true nature. This finding of your true self is paramount.

This reminds me of the story of an eagle who was raised by a flock of hens and so it could never fly to the heights that an eagle should. One day, it sees an eagle flying in the sky, yet it does not attempt to fly as it appraises itself as a chicken and underestimates its own potential.

Not diagnosing the nature of your authentic self undermines your true potential. While you could be an expert in the subject or field that you are working in, you may not be touching the fire which is dormant within you. It may go unrecognised, unutilized. That creates a sense of discontentment. You deprive yourself of the sense of joy that you were meant to feel and enjoy.

That is how crucial it is to find your own authentic self!

Finding One's Authentic Self

How Do I Find My Authentic Self?

It's a lengthy process. It cannot be understood immediately in a day or two, and yet if you wish and you really wish it clearly, it will unfold in front of you effortlessly, with ease and you will get a sudden sense of ecstasy. You will feel light, as if you have returned to the place where you truly belong. And this sense of belonging puts you in that zone where you feel yourself as free on your own, at your best. It is a moment of eureka, of sheer joy. When you find it, you have no doubt about it. You simply know that 'it is, what it is'.

There is a secret to finding this place of happiness, to be aware of your own emotions that you feel while doing anything that you are doing. Whenever you do something out of inauthenticity, it doesn't feel right, and in your heart you know it. It stresses you out, you have apprehension, you feel like running away from that situation. It does not give you the joy of fulfilment. Whereas, when anything, however small it may be, comes from your authentic self it lights you up. Lights up your heart. You feel good about yourself.

Emotions are like the guiding star in finding your authentic self. Use them to your advantage. Pay attention to them closely, especially when you face negative emotions such as anger, guilt, sadness while you do something that is not coming from authenticity. Because when you do those things that you really like you will feel happiness, joy, ecstasy, and peace. Monitor what you feel, and you will find the right way.

In life, especially in today's world where out of practical purposes we need to fulfil certain duties, follow some tasks with discipline in order to make a livelihood, there can be a question that arises: should I leave what I am doing completely and go find what I really want? When such questions come, the choice becomes individual, for responsibilities are also individual. You need to ask this question to yourself before asking anyone else: do I have the courage, do I have the guts to do it? If your heart says yes, you can follow it. But the practical suggestion could be that you can continue your livelihood while slowly and steadily shifting towards what you want. Time here is not a constraint. If you are meant to achieve something, you will achieve it in due course. Patience and perseverance are required when you decide to do something. You must ask your mind if you are strong enough to pursue it. For if this life is yours, learn to own your decisions.

There is a term called destiny. Everyone is destined to do something in life to attain a particular fruit. They have a role to play for themselves and for others who they meet in their lifetime. Whether to go on that journey or not, whether to make it better or not, it is solely a choice. Whether to make a choice or not is also a choice. Therefore, you need to make it consciously!

I remember the story of Sage Valmiki from ancient Indian history. He was once a robber and used to kill people & loot them. After realising that what he was doing was wrong, he left his wrong deeds behind and did years of *tapasya* (penance) and went on to become a great Sage called Maharshi Valmiki who wrote one of the greatest epics, the Ramayana.

This realisation and the decision to pursue one's calling, of finding your authentic self can make you a great being elevated from your ordinary, meagre life.

Will My Suffering End When I Find My Authentic Self?

To speak the truth, it does not disappear completely, but it stays, lingering, trying to haunt you as it used to before. But your response to it changes. It does not disrupt your inner peace. Your progress goes on, on the intended path. You continue in your endeavours. Outcomes do not overtly bother you as you live in the moment, the moment of being yourself and not what the world thought you are supposed to be. You start loving yourself anew. That glow in you, that shine in you cannot go unnoticed. You utilise your maximum potential. You become who you are really meant to be. You are attentive to yourself, groom yourself. You do what makes you feel excited. In the process, you share this joy with those around you and they also start becoming like you, more aligned to their own self.

This is the alignment of your body, mind, and soul which is the actual purpose of life. When everyone has attained such alignment, the earth will be a more suitable place to live for every creature, as it will help everyone attain a higher level of consciousness.

Doesn't Aligning Yourself to A Purpose Mean that You Should Keep Yourself Away from Material Life? Isn't Loving Yourself More Selfish Then?

The body given to us is an instrument, a vessel for the soul – a temple, a home where we live. Don't we take care of every temple/ religious place or our own home, to make it a suitable place for us to live in, so that it remains in an optimal condition? We feel better in a place that is clean, beautiful, full of love.

Imagine the experience we have when we go to a place of worship. We first see the beauty of it with our eyes. When we enter inside, we feel its tranquillity, we discern a certain power that dwells within and its divinity. The body in which we live is a home for our soul, then how can being solicitous of the well-being of our bodies be a selfish act? Don't we do the servicing of the instruments, machines, and cars to maintain them well? Don't we paint our house, repair it to keep it in a good condition? Similarly, we must ensure that the abode that our soul has been given during this lifetime is healthy, happy and at peace. Nourishing and cherishing our own body cannot be selfish or sinful in any way.

It is not forbidden to do things that make yourself happy, even if it means relishing food or having a luxurious life or material things. We are born here in this world to live while feeling 'ALIVE' and not for sacrificing our needs and suffering from self-pity. Any such experience leads to unfulfillment and traps one into lower vibrations. Feeling and living in abundance is not a sin, just as going after material things or earning money is not prohibited. At the same time, one must be vigilant of causing no deliberate harm to nature or people or creatures around oneself. Opting for the options that are more friendly for the environment, not causing destruction in places where we live and not harming others when we pursue our own wishes is indispensable. Realising the boundary between need and greed, and the optimal utilisation of what we earn is important.

Staying in the Present Moment

Our mind is a constant furnace like that of an atomic reactor. It enables a chain of never-ending, constant mind chatter, which all of us have inside of our head about people, situations, things, desires. It makes individuals restless, engrossed in the thought world that takes them nowhere but mis balances and disharmonizes, reducing their productivity. This string of thoughts is unproductive and thus needs to stop somewhere. You cannot get answers to any questions among this battery of thoughts because the answers you need reside in the stillness of your mind. That stillness has all the answers for you. But the real problem is that we cannot access it when we are incessantly thinking.

Staying in the present moment helps get rid of these thoughts. It means being fully present while doing everything, paying full attention to each and every act. Whether you are breathing, eating, singing, or doing any work, you must watch yourself at each step of your actions at every moment. When we are present in a moment in our full awareness, unnecessary thoughts fall off. They do not bother; they do not come. The mind accesses the peace that lies within it. Being present is a thoughtless state. The only aspect that works is awareness. For instance, if you are sitting still, experience every breath that you are taking in, paying full attention to your surroundings, to its beauty, the environment, the ambience, the temperature. If you are listening to music, immerse yourself in the melody, the words, and the instrumental play.

If you can keep yourself fully engaged in the present moment, in the now, you forget about the past and the future. It is almost always the case that people dwell in the past or the future, which they cannot do anything about.

'Now is an eternal space where life unfolds.' - Eckhart Tolle.

With each passing moment, the present moment becomes the past and future events become the present. There is no scope for anyone to stay in the past or to visit the future. What is there, what is real, what eternal truth there is, is in the now. If we do not start living in the now, then when?

Worries and pain rarely come from the now; they come from thinking about what did not go well in the past or worrying about what will happen in the future. In this thought process, we spend most of our life feeling terrible about ourselves. When we consider the now, we should ask, is there any problem in our 'now', in the present moment, whether we are alive, breathing, if we are earning enough to feed ourselves well, if we have a place to live. With this perspective one realises that there is no physical entity that is present as a problem in the now. The rest of the emotional drama that is caused by our mind while dealing with others is just an action-reaction sequence.

If we avoid an action that can cause a reaction or a reaction to an undesirable action, life will be much easier. For peace lies within our own mind and the source of conflict is also our own mind. It is a matter of what we choose – peace or conflict. If we stop reacting to outside drama, it won't lengthen and would eventually disappear. It is simply a matter of making right choices.

The first right choice is staying in the present moment and second is consciously choosing peace over conflict.

And when to do this?

As it is said in the Bhagavad Gita:
Kal kare so aaj kar,
Aaj kare so ab,
Pal me parlay hovega
Pher karega kab.

It means:

What you are planning to do tomorrow, do it today, what you are planning to do today, do it now. If the world happens to get destroyed in the next moment, then you will never be able to do it.

Therefore, make these two choices 'now' for yourself.

Let me be
In this moment
As a tiny dot
Under the vast sky
Listening to the
Melodies of heaven
Riding on a purple
Unicorn
Gliding all along
Let me caress the
Fluffy white clouds
Shining with the
Lining of silver
Soft as feather

Let me catch
My breath
When I witness
The beauty that is
Exquisite
Let me be here

In this moment
That is
Calm, serene
Still
Let me
Wet my soul
In this elixir
Replenish
Rejuvenate
Let me be
Here
In this
Dream..
For now...
For a while…

How Do I Access this Stillness by Being in The Present Moment?

By purely being an observer of the present moment, feeling the present moment, feeling the most beautiful thing that humans are gifted with. No, it's not thought, it's feeling, the awareness of feeling. Have you ever closed your eyes and tapped into the feeling of beautiful, delicate flowers? In that moment, when you are feeling, you forget your thoughts momentarily. When a beautiful butterfly passes in front of your eyes, when in a hot environment you get a breeze of cool air from nowhere. When you smell petrichor – the smell of wet soil after the first drop of rain. When you see the infinite sky filled with countless stars. When you witness the calm waves of a sea. When you sit under a tree with birds chirping on it. That momentary trance of a no-thought zone, of pure feeling, pure being is the best in order to tap into your stillness.

This time of exhilaration, of the realisation about the greater truth will expand as you try to be and stay in it perceptibly. In the moment when thoughts ensue into your mind, you can let them flow and observe, do nothing. These thoughts can be of happy moments, achievements, love, hatred, anger, sadness, betrayal, jealousy, or other people's judgement over you. Various sentiments will arise when these thoughts wash over. Observe what you feel, observe what you do – you may burst into laughter, you may smile, your eyes may get welled up with tears that start trickling over your face. You may feel their wetness. You may feel anger, the muscles of your face may become tense. But only observe, don't react, don't force them to stop. Let everything come out slowly. And then let go of what was troubling you. Just let it leave your system, your mind, your heart.

Emotions are not bad per se, however, comprehending all the emotions we feel is an illusion, an illusion created by the drama of this illusory world that we live in, that we know is perishable and how one day we are not going to be part of it all. What we encounter or sense in any moment is going to pass with that moment and every moment gives us new experience in a new way. When we grasp this truth, we become the master in letting go of the attachment of that self-loathing, bringing ourselves into a state of inner peace where no obstacles can cause trepidation within us, where no emolument makes you jump with joy. You become complacent with your own being. Nothing disrupts the essential acclamation that lies within you, that state of equilibrium where you do not require people for validation, where you feel complete within yourself, where your search for something that you always felt was missing, disappears. You realise you do not have to find it outward in other people, in the outer world, for it is eternally present in you wherever you go, and whatever you do it goes with you, it stays with you. At that point, the sense of separation from the world drops. That sense of fear of the unknown goes away. You realise that everything that ever existed and does exist is connected with each other like a chain; everything is interlinked. The whole world becomes your home. The boundaries that are created by cast, creed, society, and nation are mere namesakes. Everything, and everyone is united. This united consciousness imbues you with love. You vibrate at the highest frequency of abundance. You become transparent. Everything that happens to you passes through you without disturbing your core. However, reaching this place, staying there, maintaining, or holding on to it is a tough task. Still, if there is will there is a way.

When you tap into the frequency of abundance you feel the love for every being around you. You feel connected to everyone.

You also forgive the people who have harmed you, belittled you, who were rude to you. At this point, you forgive yourself too. You don't need to purposely strive to forgive anyone. It comes automatically without any effort. This effortless state is crucial, as when it transpires that there is surrender, complete loss of resistance, there is transmutation of those negative feelings.

Though in the initial period of this state, there will be a to-and-fro movement, a moment of complete forgiveness to a profound hatred. But don't judge, observe. Let it flow. When you pay attention to it, you realise that this feeling of hatred is an illusion, it is a drama created by your own mind towards external circumstances which are already part of the past and cannot be changed. If there is still any scope of improvement in the situation, it can be attempted, however, if there is none then holding a grudge in our mind is hurtful to no one else but to ourselves.

Hatred or grudge is a kind of emotion that binds us from being our good self, doing good action, being calm, peaceful or happy. It's like a prison behind which you feel entrapped, far away from a better version of yours, from your own well-being. Whether you want to remain in the prison created by your own mind or you want to feel free within yourself, it is totally your own conscious choice, again! You have free will. When such kind of hatred or grudge tries to entrap you it is important to become cognizant in that moment – close your eyes, inhale deeply, be mindful of your own breath, feel the temperature of air coming in, till which part of your body this breath is going, how your stomach and chest are expanding outside when you breath in and falling in when you breath out. Do it for a few breaths till you feel a bit relaxed, until your focus shifts from those negative thoughts of hatred or anger. Now when the thought vanishes, open your eyes, look around whatever you see, observe with complete focus, and bang! You are on the right track again!

Our mind is like a toddler, a restless child. It will always try to pull you towards negative emotion, and so in order to generate positive emotions, you need to take extra efforts. Mind wants to keep you idle at rest. So, you become smarter. Reduce your overactive negative thinking mind by being in the present. Put those negative thoughts at rest. Let your consciousness arise over the mind.

Sitting still in the moment
Feeling the gentle breeze across your face
Breathing air while observing it
Flowing in and out of your body
Smelling the aroma around
Seeing the beauty around
Not just seeing but absorbing it
In soul through the windows of your eyes
Touching your hair
Hearing the soft rustle when you move your
Fingers through
Realising how perfect you are in your own being
Being happy with yourself
Not relying on anyone else to make you happy
Understanding that you are the sculptor of your own world
You are the lead and no one else
It's you who is important
It's you who is amazing
How wonderful life is
When everything starts from you
And everything you want comes to you
Being grateful to the creator
For making you who you are.

How are The Mind and Consciousness Different?

Your consciousness is your divine light, the essence of your primary existence, without which there is no life. It is attuned with the creator, with the highest good. It always helps to perform at a higher state of emotions whereas the mind can function at both higher and lower states. It is mainly in survival mode, carrying daily activities for your own welfare even if it means disrupting others, and your surroundings.

Why Does the Mind Try to Tap into Lower Emotions?

The brain invariably likes to do things with minimum effort. It wants to reduce its activity, to stay in its comfort zone. Once we set about to do anything or learn anything, the brain adjusts itself to such a level that it does not have to function much for that once learnt task. There are several examples of this – walking, running, climbing steps, driving, swimming, cooking, and working on a computer. It is a way of conservation of energy so that humans can multitask at the same time and do not require the same level of concentration every time they do the same task.

At the same time the brain also tries to shield you from plight, which is registered as a threat, like going on stage, public speaking, swimming for those who have a fear of water, etc. While this protective response can be good in a child, where they get scared of fire when they get burnt, it is not advantageous in every scenario, as largely the events that are perceived as a threat by the brain are not so in reality. Yet, the brain fabricates a farce for you to not do those things. It restricts the growth of an individual, as such a response abandons you from risk taking, playing around possibilities, grabbing opportunities. Similarly, when an adversity occurs, the brain takes a shortcut to overcome it to avoid the pain that could be inflicted by this event. It tries to avoid situations, by choosing every other thing in order to give temporary feelings of well-being.

Whenever there is shock, there is a trigger of events in the brain. It goes through five phases:

- Denial: This can't be happening!
- Anger: Why did this have to happen?!
- Bargaining: Bargaining over your own values to undo the event.
- Depression: the gloom that comes from having to accept it so quickly.
- Acceptance

Any kind of emotional trauma activates pain within us while we undergo all these stages. An activation of the pain body within us is a kind of energy that feeds on emotional pain. The Pain body wants to persist, it makes you think that pain is a natural way of living; it glorifies pain. You always try to find excuses to stay sad, sullen. It relates every experience to pain even when it is not necessary. It's analogous to an addiction to pain, the feeling of victimisation of oneself. All this is a trap built by the brain that does not let us emerge from this trauma.

Emotions that arise in this state can be polar opposites such as extreme sadness, numbness, apathy, confusion, lack of focus, insecurity, fear, anxiety, jealousy, violence, anger, and irritability. All these cynical emotions are not part of our natural sense of being. When these emotions appear & take charge of the body, it manifests in different ways like loss of appetite, loss of weight or overeating, increased weight, sleeplessness, overworking, not performing well, reduced productivity, etc. The brain tends to dwell in the initial four stages of trauma for a long time unless you make a conscious choice to come out of it.

Fear is the most common after effect after a particular traumatic event. The brain generates various kinds of fears to avoid traumatic situations which are alike. Many people have different kinds of fears, mainly related to traumas they have had in the past such as rejection, abandonment, judgement, public speaking, of water, of heights, closed spaces, of the dark, and many more unimaginable things.

When fear strikes someone, the brain goes into fight or flight mode by activation of the sympathetic system. In both kinds of reactions with similar bodily symptoms, there is increased heart rate, rapid breathing, flushing of skin, tremors. If one does not try to face the situation and runs away from it, it is in flight mode and when one consciously chooses to fight the situation and overcomes the fear, gets past it, and starts developing courage to face such kinds of episodes, it is in fight mode. As the saying goes, 'There is victory ahead of fear'.

To understand fear let us know the mechanism of what exactly happens in a state of fear.

When any situation is perceived as a threat, a part in the brain called the amygdala comes into action, which further involves the hippocampus in a sequence of actions that interpret the fear. There is also the release of stress hormones like cortisol & adrenaline, which cause:

1. Increase in blood pressure
2. Faster breathing

3. Increased attentiveness
4. Sweating
5. Slowing down of the digestive system
6. Dilatation of pupils

Most of us don't realise that fear is not just mental, it is a powerful primitive response of the body which leads to all the above-mentioned symptoms.

The Purpose of Fear

Fear prepares you to deal with situations you're subjected to. It equips you to "Fight or Flight".

When your heart rate and blood pressure increases, more blood supply goes to muscles so that you can fight or run away. Elevated breathing ensures that you get an ample amount of oxygen. The slowing of the digestive system allows your body to dedicate more energy towards the task that you are involved in. Thus, you are ready to fight or flight depending upon what you choose.

This response was lifesaving in the ancient days when humans lived as hunter-gatherers, and were subjected to life-threatening situations every now and then. This "fight or flight" response helped them stay alive as the threats then were actually life threatening and the response needed had to be immediate as a few seconds of delay could lead to loss of life.

Whilst this response is of an undeniable and utmost importance in real, life-threatening situations, today such kind of situations are not as recurrent. Yet, there are certain types of fears that our mind tries to trap us in.

One universal fear is the fear of the unknown. In human beings, this fear takes the form of three main fears and the rest all types of fear are secondary to these fundamental fears:

- Fear of death
- Fear of abandonment
- Fear of failure

Any fear that is related to potential bodily suffering – disease, trauma, losing of loved ones, accident, closed spaces, height, water, etc. are in reality, the fear of death.

Any fear that is related to rejection, humiliation, ending up alone are due to fear of abandonment.

The fear of getting low grades, failing in a particular task, fear of public appearances are due to fear of failure.

How this Fear Affects Our Lives

In earlier days, when the living conditions of a large group of people were not as favourable as they are today, death was widely accepted as a natural phenomenon. But with the advent of modern medicine, where the chances of survival in any condition are better than they were before, acceptance of death is almost always denied, which has led to more lawsuits against the medical fraternity.

Technology has made our lives easier but at the same time it has put a lot of constraints on our lives, especially related to time and being with loved ones. With increased workloads, people are not able to spend time with their loved ones and on top of that, due to social media and the internet, people live virtually more than in real lives where you can be with a person as per your convenience. You are not liable for any responsibility of theirs. But this has led to extremely weak foundations for relationships – real as well as virtual – leading to an overall increased fear of abandonment or ending up alone in human beings as a whole. This leads to relationship problems such as sabotage of relationships, relationship hopping, self-victimisation and narcissism.

- Relationship sabotage: When there is fear of rejection, you try to get out of the relationship before the other person does and thus try to have an upper hand and console yourself saying that it is you who has first taken the step to break up.
- Self-victimisation: It overlaps with all the three fundamental fears. It is assuming yourself to be powerless against your worst fear. For example, blaming others for your own mistakes, not accepting your own weak points. This also leads to narcissism. Fear of failure, of being less than someone else leads you to be more vulnerable to people's judgement, depriving you from reaching to your fullest of potential by giving your best.
- Narcissism: It is also due to fear of failure and is a coping mechanism. A narcissist believes that they are not capable of failure & if it happens it is not due to their own fault but because of someone else. This makes them go into denial mode.

And then there is the less dramatic expression of fear of failure in the form of perfectionism and workaholics. They often come forward as heroes. They overcompensate their fear by putting in extra effort everywhere. They think that they can beat every failure by going the extra mile and in a way they forget that failure too is a part of life, and you cannot deny failure. In fact, pursuit of perfection is fruitless, as no one can be completely perfect. It can only lead to a maddening effect on individuals.

In most cases, the emotion of fear is erected by the mind, it is a mechanism to keep oneself safe, within a comfort zone. One can choose to stay in that comfort zone or to challenge and come out of it.

Another most important emotion that appears after any trigger or shock is anger.

Anger is a reaction to and distraction from inner suffering. It is a coping mechanism to distract yourself from what lies beneath – feelings such as sadness, inadequacy, shame, isolation, anxiety, powerlessness. It tries to distract from the intense pain that is arising from these feelings. It is a result of underlying depression.

The areas in the brain that are stimulated by anger are similar to fear. Initially, the amygdala and hypothalamus & then parts of the prefrontal cortex also play a role in anger. On potential stimulus, similarly to fear, there is a release of cortisol & adrenaline. Anger also subjects you to the fight and flight mechanism, pretty much like fear.

The defence mechanism, however, that is involved in anger is displacement, where an angry person transfers negative feelings or emotions to another person or thing considering them that they are responsible for the situation.

An anger arousal cycle has five phases: Trigger, Escalation, Crisis, Recovery, and Depression.

- Trigger: It is any incidence that leads to the start of an anger cycle. A trigger could be in the form of an argument, information that is unexpected, a shock, any threat. Our physiological system then prepares us to meet that threat.

- Escalation: When the body prepares us to give a response to the trigger in the form of rapid respiration, increased muscle tone, flushing, louder voice, and increased blood pressure.
- Crisis: It is when our survival instinct takes the driver seat, and picks the actual fight or flight response. Our body takes up action in this phase. Our judgement ability is significantly reduced and cloudy at this stage.
- Recovery: It takes place once some action has taken place. The body starts to recover from the extreme stress and expenditure of energy. The adrenaline in your blood starts to leave gradually. The ability of judgement returns at this stage and reasoning begins to take over the survival response.
- Post-Crisis Depression: This is the point when the body enters a short period in which the heart rate reduces below normal so the body can regain its balance. It leads to awareness and allows us to assess what just happened, leading to emotions such as guilt, regret, or depression.

Anger not only causes troubled relationships but also has physical effects such as anxiety, high blood pressure, and headache.

Whether to emerge out of a traumatic event or not is completely a question of free will. You cannot be in a state of this low vibration emotions for a lifetime. If you have a problem that needs to be addressed, you ought to face it, and attain triumph to regain a state of peace and joy. This requires acceptance at each state. For it is 'your brain' versus 'your brain' – a brain which wants you to plummet down versus a brain that wants you to upsurge. It is a choice to be made: the conscious brain or the unconscious brain.

Happiness is going out to play
Dirtying your hands in clay
It is in wearing your favourite clothes
Also in tasting sour lemon
And when randomly you dip your feet in
Lake that soothes you
It's in long, hot water showers
Shouting loudly from a tall tower
Happiness is in spending time
With those you love
And also in caring for yourself
When you feel alone
Happiness is in the gentle breeze
And in watching the sunset from
That same old bridge
It also lies in your eyes
When tears trickle down from their corners
Happiness is always in your heart
For that is your natural being
It is in small and simple things
It is when you are true to yourself
And with all those around you
When your heart feels with compassion
And with gratitude
It is in your prayers

And under all the layers
That you immerse yourself in
All you need to do is
Find it within… Find it within…

Acceptance By Being Aware of Patterns of Negative Emotions

Acceptance comes after the realisation of all the repetitive patterns you have undergone in life and understanding the way you react in particular situations – whether you are hyper in anger, venting it out over another person or do you run away, go into a cocoon? How do you find solace in such a situation?

Frequently, these reiterations are protective mechanisms developed from negative past experiences. These patterns are responses of a wounded inner child, which appear as a result of fear. These fears have a common origin that remain ingrained in the mind and are reactivated on revisiting that particular episode. The response to any undesirable situation is out of anxiety, and it is to avoid the pain. The mistake while handling this anxiety that any adult makes is ignoring the red flags of these symptoms, which further lead to the accumulation of these emotions to a point until the bubble bursts and causes a bigger negative impact on one's mental health, as your inner child then goes into an offensive mode to avoid this situation by running away from it or by completely shutting down into a mode of depression.

Using a healthy way to deal with this fear, by accepting and paying close attention to these emotions lets you move into the awareness mode. Being appreciative of a stage when the situation seems recurring, developing confidence that this situation is not detrimental and is just a type of experience, not the end of the world, requires training of the mind. Once your mind is sufficiently trained, you can successfully overcome this situation in a better, more mature way, helping your inner child to accept that it does not need to put on that alarm and does not need to start that protective mechanism. It is safe in this situation, assuring it that the adult you are able to take care of that vulnerable child.

When your inner child becomes reassured, it helps you accept the new situation to deal with it in a better way, as it considers that you are capable of taking care of it. One needs to take one's own time to go through this. Let the process undergo complete evolution, as it will help you evolve into a whole new personality, which is better, joyful, healthy, more efficient, more responsible, and more loved. Wherever this course takes you, this journey of healing yourself is worth taking a ride on.

There comes a time when you question everything
    everyone around you
    Including yourself
    Your old way of living no more excites you
    And you skip in a zone of silence
    Where you realise that what's happening
    That you think was troubling you
    Is nothing but an orchestrated drama
    It was all meant to happen
    You learn to forgive everyone… including you
    And then your life moves like a flow…

How to Get Rid of The Mind Trap?

The mind is a powerful tool when used correctly. However, it can be your friend or your enemy. And how it behaves depends upon how you train it. So how do you get rid of the inner demons of fear that are unnecessarily magnified by the mind?

When you're in the midst of a negative thought process, the mind makes you believe that life is about suffering and pain is the natural way of living. It tries to hold you back by creating a false sense of fear. Here, all we need to understand is that this is a pattern of the mind to keep us in the comfort zone, where it does not feel threatened. The realisation that this fear is an illusion created by the mind is necessary. At the same time, accepting that in any undesirable situation we can only put efforts to overcome it and at the same time we cannot control the outcome of any situation, is important. Most stressful emotions are created because we try to imagine the outcome of any situation and we often imagine it in a negative way. This creates a sense of fear that gives rise to an unbalanced response. An action that happens in response to fear in an unbalanced state of mind creates undesirable results, leading to a vicious cycle. Hence, being in an utmost state of awareness – that we can control only our actions and not the reaction of anyone else, nor the outcome of any situation helps to break the chain of negative patterns.

A lazy mind will tell you not to exercise in the morning, reminding you how tired you are and by giving you hundreds of reasons. A fearful mind will tell you how a particular situation is not favourable for you and will project risks involved as huge ones deterring you from taking up a new task. But when you train your mind optimally by regular practice of meditation and mindfulness, the mind becomes your friend and makes decisions in the favour of your growth.

The Mind and Mental Health

Why is Taking Care of The Mind Necessary?

Our mind is the one that drives the body to take action, to do things. If the mind is healthy, it will manifest a healthy reality. If it is sick, it will manifest as an unhealthy one. Many people these days are taking care of their bodies with diverse exercise routines and diet plans. They are taking care of their looks with various beauty products and designer wear, and of their surroundings by beautification. Nonetheless, their real abode where they live their whole life, the one that drives their life, their mind, is customarily left uncared for, unnourished for.

The mind is an entity which is not seen even though throughout our life it undergoes various traumas. Everyone has their own adequacy to deal with these traumas. It's like different skin colours – darker skin tones that have higher amounts of melanin can withstand sunlight for longer durations without much damage to skin, whereas lighter skin tones that have lower amounts of melanin can bear sunlight only for shorter durations. It reacts with redness when the intensity or duration of sunlight increases as its resistance against sunlight is less.

Likewise, some people have thick skin to face difficulties and traumas. They are more resilient. On the other hand, there are some who have a tender heart, so they are more sensitive to the situations around them. At times they get affected by the emotions of others' too. Some people care for people more than they care for themselves. They love their loved ones so much that they forget their own value at times. Such people have to be more careful with their mind and their heart, as they are the most vulnerable.

If the mind is left uncared for, there is an entrapment of negative emotions and energy, which leads to various lifestyle diseases such as diabetes, hypertension, autoimmune diseases. If you forget to, or avoid taking care of your mind, beware, it's not just about your mind but your body too. A restful, healthy mind is required for a healthy body.

It is commonly believed that sudden emotional shock can shoot up blood pressure, which can lead to a heart attack, brain haemorrhage, or paralysis. And this occurs when you have not trained your mind to control your emotions.

Sadness can also cause physical damage to the muscles of the heart as well, which can lead to heart diseases and at times death. It's important to take care of your mind if you desire a healthy functioning body free of diseases.

A healthy mind creates a healthy energy field around it. Everything in the world is energy living or nonliving, vibrating at certain frequencies, attracting people and objects of similar frequencies. Animals are sensitive to energies too. When anything wrong is about to happen, they can sense it. It is also referred to as 'sixth sense' or 'intuition'. Few human beings do have a strong sense of intuition. Similarly, as we experience many times in real life, when something good is about to happen, it happens with a series of good things. When bad things happen, it also flows in the same pattern. Everyone is attracted to things and experiences based on their energy field. Hence, the stronger your mind is, the stronger your energy field is and vice versa.

We unnecessarily harm the health of our mind by unintentionally engaging into practices that damage our own self worth. Let us re-evaluate a few habits and definitions. For instance, repetitive use of the word 'sorry'. While saying sorry for genuine mistakes is necessary, one must understand it does not reduce the gravity of the mistake. It might reduce the burden that you feel in your heart, whether you get your forgiveness or not.

Saying 'sorry' for a mistake that has happened for the first time can be admissible but when the same mistakes are repeated and the sorry is said to seek forgiveness, the word loses its weight. Also, sometimes one gets into the habit of saying sorry as a part of keeping another person in their life, by pleasing that person's ego. In such situations ,apology comes even without one's mistake, and that is harmful for one's own mental health.

At times, people are generous enough to forgive when you say sorry. Many times though, your apology nourishes the feeling of their own grandiosity in their mind. They expect it to come each time they want it and try to use manipulative tactics. If you keep on saying sorry for trivial things, it reduces your value in people's eyes, not to mention your own eyes. You develop a sense of low self-worth, devaluing your worth in your own mind. It puts the other person on a pedestal and you at the bottom. It ruins your self-respect.

Then should we not say sorry? Offering an apology depends upon the situation. Sometimes people say sorry even though they are not feeling so. An apology should be offered only when you yourself feel it is right to say sorry, as it is worth offering only if it is genuine.

Proving Yourself

The whole system is about proving yourself – that you are better than others, you are perfect. There is a constant race of proving yourself in society, first by your parents and then by yourself.

Should you fail, people call you lame and worthless. And we fall prey to the opinions of other people and furthermore try to keep on proving ourselves in front of them even if it is not necessary, even if it is not working. Deliberately pushing yourself into doing anything, just to prove to a handful of nuisance-creating people in society will stress you out without your own awareness. At a certain point you will be working or doing things just to prove that you are worthy enough.

You must think, who are these people? A group of souls unsatisfied with themselves that they could not achieve a certain position in their lives and that they have time to judge others. Is it really necessary to give those faceless people with baseless allegations the right to affect you? Many people think that the rules of society are measures to keep the system in check. But blindly following something just because someone told you to and moreover, following a whole lifestyle merely to fulfil the rulebook of society, doing things that don't satisfy your own zest towards life at times can be very difficult. Continuing such a way of life builds mental pressure, for not everyone is good at every single thing. Some will be good at studies, some at arts, some in architecture, some in sports, some in singing, and so on. Following one's innate desire of doing what you are good at, what satisfies you without trying to prove yourself to anyone, only to enjoy the journey, can not only give you mastery in that subject but it also gives you a sense of peace.

However, if we continue to be under mental pressure of being judged by people in the name of system standards, we can hardly perform well. We need to realise that life is not a race, and we are not a herd of sheep. Everyone can do well in the subject that they are good at. Observing, searching passionately what really inspires you, exploring all the dimensions that excite you to find that one thing can go a long way to improve your perception of life. As if you are good at something naturally you will do it in a better way, and it will give you a sense of harmony about your life.

Only a calm mind which is balanced can perform optimal work and only that kind of work can create good results. When a task is performed under pressure, even if we initially feel that the result is good, ultimately it collapses after a certain point of time because that weak link in vibrational alignment does not let the structure get stability. Therefore, balancing your energies, aligning them to the highest frequency of joy and ecstasy is necessary when you want a certain thing to work out in a certain way. When you do a particular thing to prove yourself without your own wish, only because others are doing it, you get affected by the judgement of other people, and this way, you can never achieve good results, plus no satisfaction. Hence, freeing yourself from the burden of judgement is of the utmost importance, more than anything else, even before starting any of the work.

If We Don't Work to Prove Anything, What Motivation Can We Have to Improve?

Any work can be done in a fruitful way if you feel good about it. No work can be done by clinging to a peculiar result in mind. This is a challenging concept to understand. It isn't about not setting a goal to accomplish a desired result. It is about releasing the attachment with that goal. When we are desperately attached to a specific goal, it creates a sense of anxiety, which pushes this goal further away from us. Instead, we can keep creating an environment of positivity and work towards it. There is creation of all possibilities that this thought can come to fruition at the same time when we think it. Only the time period, the struggle, the path towards it and the possibility of it not coming into reality depends upon our attachment pattern. A conscious healthy attachment pattern creates a positive healthy process which follows the fruition of thought into reality in a more positive way. Whereas, the anxious attachment pattern produces unhealthy cords that lengthen the process and can make the outcome negative and painful.

The motivation in any thought to come into fruition should be a joyous process, dedication to the process, and not solely to the outcome.

Being True to Yourself

Every soul is like an element in nature. The elements – air, water, soil, and fire – have their own properties that cannot be changed. If we look at it more scientifically, each element, be it solid, liquid, or gaseous, has particular properties owing to which they maintain a particular form. Even when they react with other elements, the type of reactions and their outcome is fixed. What compounds they will form with other elements is fixed. Such is the case and the whole system is that sophisticated, even if we think about giant, heavenly bodies that are present in this infinite space that rotate at a specific speed on a specific axis, moving in a specific orbit, at a specific distance from other bodies. What happens when there is a change in any of these parameters? Even if it is miniscule, it can cause destruction, not only of that giant body but other surrounding structures too.

Similarly, when it comes to this, it follows laws that are defined by nature – divine power as we may call it. Then how can the thing that we cannot see yet be an essence of every being which we call soul, and not follow the inherent nature of it? How do we even think that it is possible?

In Indian astrology, depending upon the time of birth of every human being, a birth chart is prepared, which predicts the future of that being. There are different calculations made to predict the inherent nature of that person along with the future events that are going to take place in their life. There are different parameters that are used to predict the very nature of human beings such as planetary conditions, constellations, zodiac signs, *gan*, *nadi*, *yoni* & many more. This correlation is accurate in most of the cases though not in entirety. If we try to analyse it, it could be one of the ancient sciences that define and assess the fabric of that particular being.

However, what exactly is the nature of a soul is difficult to assign. Yet, it gives an idea as to why two siblings reared in the same family, in the same belief system, the same societal pattern can be poles apart in their demeanour.

We often think children whom we have borne are our responsibility, they should be just like us or as we want them to be. They should follow rules that we think are right or our way of life. While doing this, we often forget the free nature of every soul. Each soul will behave according to an elemental tendency that has woven its fabric, no matter how much we try to revise it. Sooner or later it will align itself on the path of its nature. When such is the case, it is an illusion to say, "I disciplined my child, I am the one who has created my child. I have carved their future." In reality, each parent is a medium, a supporter but the creator of every individual is the person themself. No matter how good your values are, the child will adapt to those values only if it follows their own basic nature, their soul.

So when it comes to raising a child, you just need to monitor emotional impulses, because the brain of a child cannot make decisions using their impulses. You can tell them the values you have. But whether they will follow the exact same values or not depends on the yearning of their soul. You cannot hold them responsible if they do not turn out exactly like you. You cannot instil something in them, from an external source, and see it grow within them, until there is that inner urge, an inner fire that is lit from the source of the person.

If we condition a lion to become a cow, what destruction are we causing it? We are killing the lion's potential to rule. And, if we are conditioning a cow to become a lion, we are killing its potential to nurture or to love. We are not creating the future, we are moulding it in breakable plastic, which ultimately causes chaos, dissatisfaction, and collapse. Do we really aspire to do that? Of course not. We cannot impose someone to do something, just as we cannot impose ourselves to do something only because someone told us to do it. It's about respecting boundaries, abilities, and hidden qualities which will shine when given a chance to exercise, when explored.

She was chained She was drained
It was difficult for her To follow the rules
For her heart always Wanted to dance in rains
She kept trying harder To be like others
Only to realise That it made her suffer
One day she decided To break the barriers
And to follow What she desires
And now she was free To dance in the rains
Dance in the Rain…

Success

Success is a subjective term, the meaning of which changes depending upon societal belief, and where you are living. For academic people, success would mean academic success, for artists it is having mastery in their respective art, for businessmen it could be material success, for politicians it will be winning an election, for athletes winning medals. It's all about winning, having finesse in what you are doing. And that is right. You should be doing what you are doing with passion, complete dedication, and concentration. Moreover, you should be in a state of mind that helps you go further and do better in your field. Still, is that enough? Is career your entire life or it is just one part of life?

When you consider success on an individual basis what should it be?

Ideally, success should be maintaining a state of healthy mind, body and soul at any given point of time. Success is not an outward term, it is inward; when you can maintain an equilibrium of your mind, body and soul at any given point of time. When you no longer feel that life is a pressure to deal with but is a journey to enjoy, a ride worth taking. It is when you feel comfortable being in your own skin. When you accept yourself, love yourself and project that love to others with compassion, that is success.

When you attain this inward success, things become a bit easier. First thing first, you should search out the reasons within you that are stopping you from gaining what you want – whether it is a sense of fear, of inadequacy, mindset, inadequate efforts or what I am doing right now does not fit the path that I should be on. An answer to the question, 'Why am I not able to do what I am supposed to' lies within yourself. It's beneath all the layers of you, of the conditioned you. You are not supposed to ask this question to anyone else but yourself because when you ask others, the answer will come through the limited experience of that person. Limited to how much of the world that person has seen or not seen. Hence, it will always be incomplete. While they can still give you an answer, their experience may not always be beneficial for you. Their way of thinking might not give you the same results as it gave to them. Even their thinking might be outdated. When you seek answers from others to your own questions and follow their advice, and in case you fail on the way, you will end up blaming them. That means you succumb to cowardice and do not fully take responsibility for your own doing, which further pushes you from a cliff into a deep valley of negative emotions. Of course, you can take someone's guidance, but you are not supposed to be overdependent on them. Take only the things that you feel in resonance with.

Therefore, always try searching for your answer within yourself. Own your responsibility of living your own life. Once you identify the obstacle that is coming in the way of your success and once you decide that you will work to remove it, you start pursuing your decision. You take efforts, little by little every day. Every moment you get closer to the success, that in your eyes you perceive as success.

What you are outside is a mere reflection of what you are inside. When the inside world is vibrating at peace and at the frequency of abundance, for it has come closer to the natural sense of being through reflection, introspection, you will attract more abundance, more success in material terms.

All the same, what in this material world is perceived as success is more in monetary terms as to how much you are earning, what is your net worth, how many houses or cars you have, your bank balance. Well, all these things may help one feel abundant, however, the happiness or joy you gain from such outer things is temporary. It stays for a while, and then once you get used to them you get attracted to newer things available in the market. When one searches for happiness, joy, peace, and repose, and does not get it in their outward space, one then realises that all of it exists in your inner space, in your being, your soul, your essence, in the divinity of the universe that dwells within you.

Once you realise this, you begin searching inside of you, you attain a state of comfort where outward criticism or validation hardly has any impact on your mind. What you do for a living, you start doing it with more love and that in turn increases your productivity, your performance. When your productivity increases, you get more appreciation and financial gains. That is why, before searching for happiness outside, you should search it inside of you first. You must learn to be happy with your own stillness, to befriend yourself, to enjoy your own company. Instead of searching for anyone else as your best friend, become your own best friend. Admire yourself for what you are. Only when you are comfortable with who you are as a being, will you be able to be comfortable with life's challenges. You will find yourself competent and capable of attaining success.

To attain success, you need to let go of any resistance. This is the resistance of social conditioning that makes you believe you are not enough, you are not capable, you are not gifted, you are not talented enough, you are ordinary, while comparing yourself with others. This conditioning is embossed in your subconscious mind from childhood, entrapping you into a false identity, which is reflected outwards as failure.

Be conscious of the fact that every person who is considered great today was once ordinary. Not everyone is born with a silver spoon. When you say someone is ordinary it is your conditioning speaking for you, not you. Had it been your purest being speaking, you would have known that everyone, every being is a matter of energy. The energy that is universal, from the source, is the essence of source & if we consider so, it has the source within it. In that case, if everyone, everything that has a source in it, ordinary does not exist. Every being is special, as every being is divine. No one is big, no one is small, and no one is equal as everyone is unique, playing their part in the universe according to their Karma, the part they are imparted to play. For life is like a jigsaw puzzle – every piece of it has a place. If one is here, it is because one is worth being here, and has a role to play that was assigned to them. Every being is experiencing this universe with the instrument of their body. The experience can be changed provided they change their inner dialogue, conditioning, and beliefs.

Why is it Difficult to Change the Inner Dialogue?

When a child is born, it has no inner conditioning. The conditioning happens as the child grows over the years of its life. It comes from the people who surround him or her, and the experiences of those who rear them. In most cases, the conditioning that happens is fear-based because everyone the child comes across while growing up carries various unrecognised emotional traumas within them. These traumas give rise to fear as a protective mechanism to avoid the recurrence of such traumas. These fears mainly revolve around self-doubt, fear of future events, fear of rejection, fear of abandonment, fear of judgement, fear of ridicule, fear of not being enough, fear of death, fear of losing something or someone valuable, and fear of loss (physical or emotional) among others.

Every individual carries these fears in different compositions. These fears occur due to various experiences an individual gathers during their lives as well as from those who surround them. And these fear-based energies give rise to different emotions in different individuals determined by their personality. Though individuals react differently to fear, there are very few who can do something constructive through this. Emotions that surface out of fear are predominantly anger, resentment, sadness, apathy, depression, and bitterness. Fear and its secondary emotions form an insoluble chunk in one's mind, remaining there and clogging one's awareness. These changes are not recognized by people, as they do not show up until an undesirable event occurs.

These emotions also lead to diverse actions. These actions can be of one type or a combination of various types. They are a kind of protective mechanism, a shield that individuals use to protect themselves from trauma. These actions might include clinginess, a need to over explain, being apologetic for no mistake, fights, quarrels, violence, running away, not expressing feelings, and forming solid impenetrable walls surrounding oneself.

For instance, if a person is fearful of judgement of what people will say, they may not express themselves well, may not speak publicly over any subject, may not opine candidly. Other types of people bully others over their shortcomings to have a sense of confidence. They might be bitter and say rude things to others. Whenever someone is not being nice or is behaving in uncertain strange ways, it is not always that person's fault; it is their wounded self that is causing such a reaction or coping mechanism.

These things restrain the growth of an individual, which leads to dissatisfaction. It becomes a vicious cycle and turns into patterns which are difficult to break. In such a scenario a person tends to use distractions to fill the gap, such as over socialisation, substance abuse, and even violence.

Is There a Way to Break the Pattern?

Going inward, or 'Conscious Acceptance' of the pattern, the source of the problem is the principal step. If there is acknowledgement of a particular problem, there will be a conscious effort to avoid that emotion-reaction pattern that comes secondary to the deeply ingrained fears within.

This acknowledgement, however, is not as easy as it sounds. There will be a forceful effort on the body, the body that is activated after a trigger point due to any kind of fear, to retain the cycle. There will be a flood of emotions. There will be judgement by the mind on yourself and on others.

And so, now comes the next step: 'To Feel'. Feel everything, every aspect of the emotion with all its facets without resisting it. It can be excruciating and time consuming, and will feel as if there is an overflow of negativity inside of you. It may become too overwhelming at times, almost unbearable. Still, staying with the feeling is important, as once the flood passes there will be Reflection, Understanding, and Realisation of all illusions that what was happening until now was merely a lesson. It's not permanent, it will pass.

You will realise you are stronger than this test. You underestimate your power, but momentary downfalls cannot remain for a lifetime. As you've heard, 'If there is a will there is a way' but it is also true that 'If you don't have a way, start over again'. What is happening outside is nothing but drama – an illusion to test your patience. If you must pass this test, rather than changing your circumstances, change yourself. Understand your worth, love yourself, take care of yourself. If you do not befriend yourself and understand yourself, no one else will.

People always have something to say. They will say good things on your face and bad when you turn your back. They will praise you when you are there but hate you to the core. They will judge you for everything you do, not do, you say or don't say, for how you look, how you carry yourself, for your skills, for everything on the earth. It is alright if someone judges you. It is their Karma. If you get affected by their judgement and lose your composure for all that they are saying, then it means you have not worked well on yourself. Your mind should be like a deep ocean, no matter how many waves are on the surface, deep down it is tranquil, serene, calm, peaceful.

You cannot stop people from passing judgement. Arguing with them, making them understand your point of view will be of no use if they have made up their mind about a certain thing. What you can do is not let that judgement penetrate your mind. Be a mirror, reflect every judgement that comes to you, along with every praise as well.

Not getting flattered with praise is necessary too. Praise is when someone has a good feeling about you at that moment. It's a moment of extreme love and compassion. However, it does not last forever. It reduces in intensity and diminishes as well over time. When this moment passes, they might even regret the praise or may not feel that feeling in the same way as they did before. Therefore, it is better not to get carried away in this momentary praise and let it go. Do not get attached, do not let anyone's words or intentions affect your well-being. Stand in your truth, remember your truth. Do not hold on to anything too tight. Let life flow, flow in its own way, at its own pace, in its own direction like a river. When you don't hold back, don't resist, there comes a point where you reach infinite wisdom, or at least get glimpses of it. Wisdom that is so expansive yet minuscule, so complex yet simple. Wisdom about love, unity, an understanding of the presence of the divine essence in all forms that ever existed. The glimpses of this reality will be far from whatever you have perceived until now and will give you a feeling of rapture. Seeing the beauty of this truth will leave you eternally mesmerised.

Validation

Unknowingly, we all are overly sensitive to receiving validation, which is the opinion of others about our actions. Whether I am doing right, whether people appreciate me, whether my presence is liked by people, do I look good, are my physical characteristics good enough... The list is unending. The longing for this validation starts ever since the toddler age and it continues till our death bed.

Humans are social animals; they prefer to stay in groups. If one does not fit in the standards of society, how can they be part of a group? This is the prime motive for seeking validation from other people. Validation is sometimes sought for the simplest of our actions. However, we often forget that be it anyone, whether it is a great human being who is admired for their good qualities like their wisdom, courage, and valour, who has gained enormous name, fame, money, or an individual who could not attain any of it in the slightest amount, and all those ordinary people who fall between these two spectra are both hated and liked for the qualities that they have simultaneously by different groups of people. People have various reasons to like you or not like you. They might like you for selfish motives because you are useful to them in a certain way. They might like you because they seek inspiration from you. There will be others who do not find you of any use to them, they might envy you for what you have and they don't.

Validation, be it of any kind for anyone is always situational. It depends on the role of different people in that situation. People might not validate you as they perceive you as a threat. Then when we seek validation, it will be first for validation itself and then to know the reasons behind validations. Do we really need to use our time and energy for something that is so very fickle and unimportant?

Even if you may have many fallacies, you will still be appreciated by those who love you even with those fallacies. Those who hate you will hate you even for your good qualities. Great beings, deities, great inventors also could not be saved from the criticism by people around them. Because people always have something to say.

Validation by people is nothing but the projection of you in people's minds. It is not that they don't like you or hate you, it is just how they perceive you and how they respond to the image of you in their mind. These perceptions about anyone in anyone's mind often come from fear, insecurity or a block that they have in themselves. When a person is free from these blocks, they will not judge the outside projection of any person, as they do not have the time, energy and need to consider meagre things to judge others, they have compassion in them.

In that case, why seek validation of people who in their own self do not feel secure, appreciated and complete. It's not your external qualities that define who you are, it's how you are within, in your being, that defines you. Being bothered by those who are uncouth towards everyone stands no purpose.

Instead, what you can do is to love yourself for your qualities, strengthen them, and improve your fallacies, at least those that you can. There is no need for perfection. Perfection is a myth created by human beings. Everything in this universe is perfectly imperfect – the giant celestial bodies like earth and other planets, even our very own moon which shines bright in the sky has blemishes. The trees around us do not have symmetrical branches. Every leaf, every fruit, every flower is beautiful in its own way. When we embark on achieving perfection, in that very moment we lose the joy of creation, the joy of being, as the whole focus shifts into achieving perfection. While in such a case, the creation can be perfect, the process is painful. For us it is always the result, the end that we long for and deprive ourselves of the sense of ease, so that we can enjoy the process of being in the present moment. We bind all the end results into a deadline, thereby further increasing the pressure. And somewhere we miss the flow of life. We become slaves of time, machines, humans, organisations, banks, nations, the world. Still, we boast about what we have, even though we know for ourselves that what we have is a mechanical and technical thing that is deprived of feeling. It is like a glass jar which looks beautiful from the outside but empty inside. The exuberance of living life to the fullest is dampened by this compelling validation, perfection, leaving a sense of constant sogginess within.

Consider a scenario where you see a well-groomed, well-maintained garden with bushes cut in a particular shape, in a decorum on one side and on the other hand, you see a forest near a water body which has grown haphazardly with no rule, with creepers, different coloured flowers, tall and short trees of various different breeds, with varying lengths of grass. Which appearance do you find more beautiful, more soothing? Opinions on this will be different.

While talking about beauty, many will prefer the garden over the forest but when we talk about perceiving a sense that is soothing, how many will prefer the garden over the forest? The number will be less in this case. Whatever is in its natural form is more soothing to mind than the artificial one.

When one emphasises on getting validation from others, they cannot give the best out of their work as they get engrossed by the fear of failure. It comes from the feeling that what work we are doing or what new thing we are trying to do will not happen optimally. We might not succeed in it. We may not get support, and sufficient resources. It keeps us from trying new things, accepting new challenges. Fear of failure comes from a natural drive to protect ourselves from risky situations. Though it is part of the protective biological response to keep ourselves away from danger, it is not useful in situations where there is no actual threat. Whatever new thing we are trying to do or whatever work we are doing in general, not starting it or not doing it for an imaginary threat or an elusive idea that is projected by the brain can do no good to anyone.

A fear of failure can also come from negative validation by family, society. A fear that one may be judged, belittled, laughed at, and ridiculed for what we are doing. And this creates anxiety in one's mind, deterring them from doing their best. When we seek validation, we create this pressure on ourselves which creates an environment that is not suitable for healthy growth.

When we are in our natural essence, we bloom more, shine more. Hence, seeking validation is unavailing. Being yourself without the fear of judgements will be utilitarian to keep yourself at peace.

Self-Image

The idea of self-image is so delusionary because we call it self-image, and yet it is created based on the perceptions that others have about us as a person, through the eyes of others.

From the time that you are born, you grow as an individual through the rearing of those around you, their stereotypes, through culture, through society that you live in. But despite all these external things that stick to you as conditioning, there is a special essence of your own which remains present at all times with you, whether you realise it or not, whether you accept it or not.

In Hindu culture they define three ways of living life with three types of behaviours:

- Satva: honesty
- Raj: passion & activity
- Tam: destruction or chaos

'Satva' is a quality of goodness, positivity, serenity, balance, peacefulness and virtuousness that is drawn towards the others. 'Raj' is a sense of activity without any particular value that can be either good or bad. 'Tam' is the quality of destruction, lethargy, and dullness.

Everyone has a combination of these attributes with the predominance of one of these in them. All these qualities are necessary to be present as only having honesty, balance, peace without action is of no use. Doing things that are not useful or continuing doing them will not take us anywhere, hence destruction or changing the way of living in that particular area that does not serve us is also necessary to live a fruitful life. None of these attributes are inferior per se, unless they are in excess. To create balance, we need the perfect amalgamation, along with respecting what we have predominantly in ourselves.

There are certain enemies, however, of leading a fruitful life in the form of tendencies that each one has. Those are 'Kam' (desire), 'Krodha' (anger), 'Lobha' (greed), 'Mad' (arrogance), 'Moha' (delusion/excess attachment) and 'Matstara' (jealousy). They are called 'Shadripu' in Sanskrit – the six enemies. They also arise at different occasions in human beings. These all contribute to the personality of an individual.

Your self-image, what you perceive through the perception of others, which comes through your way of being with them, how you spend time with them. It can be either positive or negative, depending upon the actions you take to deal with circumstances you were facing/dealing with at a particular time. Each circumstance or incident that occurs in our life is either temporary or cyclical, rarely permanent. But the impression that it gives to other people about you and your behaviour remains permanent according to the saying, 'First impression is the last impression'. This is prejudice. And we develop a prejudice about ourselves when we are named as being a particular type of person by more individuals or groups. For example, if many people say that you are shy you become one. Similarly, if they say you are courageous or lazy or jolly or sullen or wise or foolish, you actually become one in your own eyes. This perception of others overrides our natural sense of being. Many even live with this profoundly obnoxious 'self-image', which becomes heavy for them to carry at times. It suffocates them. It creates discrepancy in their being and doing. It creates the delusion of being someone else.

It can be compared to an actual example in mythology, when Krishna was reared by his foster parents, Nand and Yashoda, who were the Mukhiyas or chief of the cow herd. They kept him safe when his life was in danger because his own maternal uncle wanted to kill him when he was born. He was the biological son of Vasudeva and Devki, who belonged to the royal family and were Kshatriya Yadavs.

There is another example in mythology – Ravana. He was son of a Hindu sage Vishrava, who was a Bramhin and Ravana grew up believing himself to be a Bramhin but he also had a lineage of Asura (demon) from his mother, of which he was completely unaware.

These are drastic & extremely opposite examples of loss of identities of one's being where overnight you become someone that you never thought of being. Or in other words we can say you become what you actually were. This realisation of one's own being in every term is an important realisation in life.

If it is you who stays with yourself in this vessel or instrument that is your body, provided as your abode by the very creator, at every single moment, all the time, from the time you were born until you die. It is you who knows the kind of situations that you have faced in your life, it is you who knows what you feel when you take a particular decision which is against other people, or the reason that you behave in a certain way in a situation. It is you who knows all your good virtues, and at the same time your own weaknesses, and not so good qualities too. Accepting what other people say about you in their limited perception, accepting the judgement that they have for you is the worst thing that you can do for yourself. If there is anything that is important in this life that you need to do for yourself, it is to come out of the self-image that is rented from others' views and explore the goodness that shines within you.

Oh dear reveal me who are you
All I can see is fancy make-up
Of emotions that you made up
To display me
I can see your smiling face
Your designer clothes that must be
Very expensive well I love to see them
And I wish if I had them
Still more than that I wish
I would have known you
A true you without all the
Veil of goodness and perfection
Are you a wise man and courageous
Or you hold fears in your mind deep down
That are just for yourself
And not for others to show
Are you so composed and careless
That you don't mind if something
Happens against your will
Or you also sob like a child for all that you need

Do you nourish our mind & soul
As your accessories

Do you really think
That it's alright to have blemishes

Unless you are a god & not human
For once take out your mask & understand
It's ok to be a human
For a man cannot be god.

What is the Purpose of Having a Strong and Real 'Self-Image'?

Most of the time, we deal with the delusional, faulty self-image imposed by others. We are afraid of people's judgement towards us. In reality, it's not the people who are judging us but it's us who are judging ourselves ultimately. This is the biggest barrier in the growth of any individual. Because if you are grown in limiting beliefs or underestimate your own potential, you will never be able to reach your full potential unless you clear the weight of what others say. And it is often a difficult, although not an impossible task. This exploration of self, this re-identification, this awakening is an important phenomenon which is a must in everyone's life to create a real, actual image that is pure, blissful and joyous, free from any ego.

This aligning of yourself with your being is also important because it creates a harmony with the world surrounding you. As a law of nature and energy, you gradually start attracting all that is in harmony with your highest energy state that you achieve. The progress you make when you are truly yourself is unmatchable. As you attract what is helpful for you to grow, this progress creates balance and a sense of satisfaction. Your search for external things for a sense of peace, harmony, joy ends and you find everything

within your core. You align with divine energy. And this energy
unfolds through your stillness, your being and creates miracles.

There will be some days when you will feel
On top of the world
That you are the best and
No one else even exists to compete
On those days you will feel at
Your happiest swollen with pride
And then there will be days
When you will feel that everyone else
But you, is the best
And goodness in you is suddenly vanished
You are nothing but a piece of paper
Which is flowing along with the wind
And everything else is controlling
The path you are taking
You will be scared and feel
That everything is over and you
Are no longer you but someone else
Then that my dear is labelled as stress
Stress is nothing but illusion of some kind
It's just a state of mind
Dust off those thoughts that pull you down
Throw off everything that makes you frown

Remember the immense strength that you have
Look back at the difficult road that you have traversed
Get up on your own with your own courage
As it's only you who can be there

No one else can take your place
Rise from that slumber of emotions
That make you feel low
For everything that you call stress
Is your reaction and not your real glow

Find that forgotten self all powerful
Who knows that what you experience
Is just a facade and not the truth
Truth is your being that is all eternal
And never ending
Wake up!
Rise to your truth and shine your light
Be your true self and fulfil the purpose of your being…

What are the Signs that Suggest You are Not Aligned to Your True Self?

When you are not aligned to your true self, no matter what you try to do, you simply won't fit in. You will try to do things to fit in, yet you will feel secluded. There will always be a feeling of being left out, being misunderstood. You will try to search for happiness by doing things that other people do, yet you will feel a mismatch, like a patch, like an alien. You have a sense of insecurity, you constantly try to prove yourself by doing things, by pleasing people, by apologising. You always blame yourself for the mistakes of others. In your own mind you will consider yourself as frugal, with no self-respect. You won't feel that you are worthy enough. You will have mood swings – at one point you will exhilarate with joy, at another there will be sadness. There will always be a sense of emptiness, as if something is missing from a jigsaw puzzle. Life will bring the same traumas over and over. This sense of insecurity is proof that you are not aligned to your own self.

Do I belong into the
world I live in
So much time has passed
Years months seconds
Have been so long
Still what bothers me
Do I belong
Where I live
People and things I love
It looks like as pure
And beautiful as tender dove
But it's not still
Everything is moving
On waves of destiny
My soul is grooving
What is it that
I am longing for
Is it material pleasure
Or it is true love

Is it an Easy Process to Explore Yourself?

Not at all. Letting go of your ego is crushing. Letting go of an identity that is covering you, holding you doggedly is a painful process. It does not happen overnight. It takes time. It creates mental confusion, irritability, and depression. You do not recognize your false self and you do not know your true self. Pain is inflicted by old trauma, and the old identity comes over the surface and overpowers the mind. Living each day becomes a task. It is like squeezing yourself through a dark, compact capsule that is squishing you, producing pain that is unheard of, unthought of. You feel that you will never pass through all this. It will persist and it will feel as if you are trapped into it forever. You don't see even a ray of light, a fragment of hope. People with whom you were comfortable for years become strangers to you. You no longer identify them. They try to help you, but you cannot explain what's happening to you. The help that they can offer is often feeble, not useful. As it is a journey of your own, happening for you, by you, through you, it is only you who can help yourself. You may get help through someone who has high vibrational alignment, through a mentor, a Guru, a guide who understands what is happening to you. This help can be in the form of literature, an experience or through your own realisation owing to how profound the experience of this self-realisation is.

Gradually, you start changing towards your natural sense of being. This change should not be resisted. If it is, then it becomes difficult to sail through the density to a higher state of consciousness.

In this journey of self-realisation, which is a continuous process, you will often shuffle between higher and lower orbits. There are times when you will feel, "why are all these things happening to me? I was alright the way I was before this." But there is no way back. And the time required to bring about that change will depend on how much your resistance to change from the old identity is.

In this journey of knowing yourself, the important step is to understand what you are not, as being someone that you are not, is the most difficult thing to do. It deprives one of their vitality, their life force. It makes them feel trapped.

We often see cartoon characters at birthday parties that are present to entertain children. They are usually adults in the disguise of that character. The costume they wear is heavy with a zip at its back. There are only a few openings to see and to breathe. They are jam packed under that heavy dress while everyone else is enjoying their presence. Do you think the one who is doing this is really enjoying what they are doing? Or are they doing it for the sake of survival?

Now compare yourself to when you are doing something that you don't like, you don't enjoy. Do you feel that suffocation within? That is what one faces when they do a mere role play for someone else. They become a puppet controlled by others for the entertainment of others. Are you really here on this earth to become a puppet? It can be acceptable for the time being, but is it easy to do it for a lifetime?

When we pretend to be someone, often unknowingly, we do that because of multiple reasons such as tradition, safety, because others are doing it, because there is nothing else to do, because it is in our comfort zone. We have all the reasons to justify what we are doing. As it seems alright, it seems natural, as we are conditioned to do things that are conventional, following the herd seems like a natural way of living. But while doing this role play, minute by minute, we are suffocating the life force that we have within.

There was an experiment done where they tried to determine the productivity of a group of people. It was noticed that those who did work that they did not like recorded lesser amounts of productivity. Similarly, one should follow the song of their soul, follow the characteristics that are truthful for their being and should not let external things influence the expression of their being. Being someone that you are not, is one of the greatest injustices in the world.

While knowing your essence is not an easy task, knowing what you are not, is a lot easier as it just doesn't feel right, you will know it from within that it is not right. Remove every layer that doesn't feel right in order to reach the core that has YOU in the purest form, in the form of gold! Cherish that YOU, grow that YOU, feel that YOU. It will be the greatest feeling in the world. It is the greatest wisdom.

If wisdom is coloured as purple
I want to feel my breath with that purple air
Reaching the very ends of the alveoli of my lungs
Going through my heart pumping into each
Vessel and capillary
Each organ and cell till the nuclei
Traversing through my nerves
Illuminating my skin
I want to capture its very beauty with my eyes
Smell its dissolute fragrance
I want to hear its pulses
Immerse myself completely
Unabashedly, insanely
In this purple breath
I want to be in it… through it… be it
For now… for then and forever and ever
Oh dear purple air take me along with you

Fill my wings with your presence
Alight me in the blue sky, making whirlwind
High… high… and high…
Till every moment I become you
Every you become I
Dissolving all
The boundaries
The illusion
The veil…

Blaming Others

In life we meet many people. Few take care of us as a responsibility, few love us, few admire us, while there are some who do not behave in a way that we consider as positive, with us. There are people who trigger us. For they have come in our life for the same thing. Those are the ties of Karma that they have with us. We often blame that this person was rude to me, was arrogant, behaved cruelly, ripped me apart. Little do we understand that those were their jobs.

Our job is navigating through their behaviour while improving ourselves and not getting stuck in the same place or going further down. It's our action on someone's trigger and not the reaction that helps us grow. As a reaction is often brisk, short term, and does not serve an actual purpose, it's always action which is constructive.

An action comes from realisation and contemplation, out of dedication and passion. In this scenario, if we think about Japan, it was financially ruined during World War II, as its two cities were completely destroyed by nuclear weapons. It had two options: to keep cribbing and not do anything constructive or to rise above the dust and fly. The people of Japan chose to ignite the fire within, to improve, to rise to new heights like a phoenix that rises from its ashes.

Thus, it is always an action to whatever you face, that leads to a positive outcome. If you are trapped in the game of blaming others, you enter victimhood and a sense of self-pity, which is often useful to gain sympathy but nothing more than that. In other cases, if you take the action to overcome negativity or weakness in you that was inflicted by other people upon you, you become an inspiration.

Pain

A very important aspect of this process of identifying yourself is pain. We often perceive pain as something that has a negative connotation, that is not acceptable, that causes suffering. We blame people, situations for our own suffering. But the actual source of that pain is ourselves, who are not ready to look into the mirror, to face the negative aspects that exist within us. No one is there to blame for the pain that we have. It is us and our ego.

Body pain arises when there is any kind of dysfunction in the form of trauma, disease, hurt. The function of pain is to bring our attention towards something in our system that is not right. In emotional well-being, the emotional pain that we get while dealing with others is primarily suggestive of the part within us that is not acting right, that is vulnerable to criticism, to circumstances, the emotional lability that we have. Thus, pain is very much required as it happens for us to act on what needs to be mended in a positive way, to recognize the actual cause and not the superficial aspects. Healing from pain leads to the correction of problems, which leads to well-being, which in turn leads to growth.

Pain often arises in difficult scenarios in everyone's life. But in individuals who are optimistic, it leads to growth. If we look at history, everyone who was great has endured pain that is often difficult to imagine. It is like the process of purifying gold or cutting of diamonds, which ultimately make them valuable.

I am on the avalanche
It's so high
I can see near me
Both mountain and sky
There is a steep fall down
Just a feet away
Cold breeze sends chill
In the spine
Scene is not so clear
It's all fog and mist
That blocks my sight
And stops the gear
Still my heart says
Go on, you are brave
Situations can be overcome
For there is victory beyond fear.
Life can be remembered
Has it carved a niche
Go ahead of any
Obstacle or cliche
You are a free soul

Who is born to fly
Sky's the limit
Your horizon lies very high!!

Determination and Commitment

Many times in life, we decide to do something. We first decide it in our mind, then we tell it to someone. More often than not, we leave it in the middle, without pursuing it any further.

There are three important steps one needs to follow if they really want to do something:

- Initiate
- Act
- Pursue

If any one of these things is missing, we cannot attain anything from thoughts that we have alone. We have to have dedication towards what we are doing. The zest of creating a new result, a new horizon in the direction of our decision. If it excites us, then we are on the right path. We must go on to find the new that comes our way.

In this case, if we are determined to find our authentic self, the one that we are in harmony with, then we must take decisions, initiate, pursue and act with dedication. We must work through the hindrances of our own mind. At times it will feel like an impossible task, that we don't want to do. But we must believe that we are strong enough, that we have that strength in our wings.

The Waiting Zone

We put ourselves in the waiting zone, often always in the way that "I will be happy if I get this", "if I pass", "if I complete this education", "if we attain that", "if we get a partner", "if we get a promotion", "if we have a kid", "if we buy a house", then a car then another car of a higher brand, another house… the list is endless.

We put ourselves in a waiting zone for happiness. We start believing that our happiness is in buying or having material things. We fail to understand the difference between pleasure and joy. Pleasure is what we get from external, material things; it is momentary, for the time being, whereas joy is what we get from within us, by living in each moment, enriching our experiences. By always waiting to be in that highest sense of joy and running behind things we postpone the feeling of goodness that we can get in the present moment.

While we are searching for this happiness outside in different people, things, and places, little do we understand that happiness is a state of being. It comes from the core. You should be happy with your sense of being. You must be in harmony with yourself. Only then will you project that happiness outward.

It's not an outside process. It is important to be happy from within, in this moment, in every 'this' moment, for what exists is only the present. Be happy right here, right now, wherever you are, in whatever you are doing; you must find this happiness now, within you. You cannot let this moment pass in waiting for things that you might feel are important now but may not feel so as time passes.

Resistance in being happy also comes from within. As we find external things to make us feel complete, this sense of missing that we are lacking something and we need to find it, is the reason that you can never feel happy. As you complete one goal, your mind assigns another goal to keep you in the loop. Therefore, getting out of the waiting zone isn't about not setting the goal, but to attach a sense of fulfilment to that goal. Losing the resistance within ourselves of "I am not worthy of being happy on my own" is necessary to break through this waiting zone.

What you want to get from life doesn't matter
It's life that wants to give you
Life's unsolved mystery
For nobody knows what's going to happen next
So does anyone who is unaware why something
Has happened in the past
What you are is just a
Puppet whose strings are
Held up high in sky
By an unknown power
Whom you cannot see
Nor can you control
What is in your hand
Is just moving forward
Going ahead without complaining
Trying hard to strive
Working on things you
Want to achieve
But it's not you who
Can decide what's next
Or whether there will be any success
After all the hard work you do

For it's the journey that matters
And what you call success
Is mere a moment
That passes with a blink of an eye
What remains behind
Is your efforts, your genius
Your hard work
And that's what really matters
So now from this moment on
Don't surrender to
Pressure of succeeding
But keep trying until
You become the best in whatever you are doing…

Patience

What exactly is patience or being patient? It is maintaining your mind at an equilibrium in any given situation. It is losing resistance or the overt attachment towards certain outcomes. Impatience is a habit that peeps in our lives every now and then, when we are stuck in traffic, when we are expecting a certain reply or an answer. The situation may be of immense importance or might carry no significance. And when things don't happen at a certain pace, in a certain way, we start losing patience. It reflects in the form of anger, stress, anxiety, or towards the other side of the spectrum in the form of sadness, depression, or apathy. Many people think that if a person is not showing any outwardly reaction, it means that they are patient, but it could be that they are not feeling good within themselves for things not happening according to their wish. This is also being impatient.

Patience is having faith. Faith can be akin to a child who is tossed in the air by their favourite person. The child is still smiling as they know that the person will catch them. The monologue within a child's mind of "I am not going to fall" is 'Faith'.

When a difficult situation hits you, you must have unwavering faith, "I am going to get through this and come out without a scratch". When you have this faith, patience comes automatically. Yet, it requires practice, training of mind that is often flickering.

Faith comes through training the mind that what happens is for our own good. If I am not able to control the outcome, the only thing that I can do is to work for what I want and not let my peace be disturbed by any outcome, whether it is in my favour or not. Because if today it is in my favour, it is good, if it is not, perhaps there is something better for me in that bag waiting for me ahead. This unshakable faith helps to lose the resistance.

Losing resistance breaks the negative pattern of emotions, brings an improvement in focus while doing any kind of work. It so happens that we wait for a specific thing to happen for so long, we try hard and yet we don't achieve it. But one day, we suddenly shift focus from that thing and bang, it happens! Why is that? It's because we lose resistance.

Resistance and lack of patience are principal barriers when it comes to growth, and achieving a goal. Patience is necessary in any situation, which comes from faith. And where does faith come from? It comes from the act of surrendering. Many talk about their achievements, denying the fact that it is the universal power who is getting things done through us. We are merely a medium. When we realise this, we go in the mode of surrendering to the divine, the universe.

We need to let go of the attachment to the outcome, and to the timeline as well. Many people set a goal that is time bound. They set a deadline for work to get done. It can be true in certain situations such as clerical work, construction or learning. More often than not, however, setting timelines creates a sense of pressure. There are certain processes that cannot work on a timeline such as creative processes. Similarly, searching for your soul also cannot be time bound. Timelines are useful to discipline the mind. Still, when used in excess, it creates a sense of being worn out. As the natural being of a soul is going in flow, timelines bind the free soul in a trap. Hence, a judicious use of timelines is necessary. It is not like one size fits all. One should be careful while doing this. As when we bind life in a timeline, there is no excitement, and no excitement means no creativity. Creation is the work of a mind that is alive. For the mind to feel alive, it must be free, following its spirit.

Don't
Don't try to be perfect…
Don't try to compete…
With anyone else or with yourself…
Don't feel bad for what you don't have…
Don't feel sad for what you could have had…
Don't cry about the past…
Don't wait for the future…
Don't think what people will say…
Don't hold back from saying what you feel…
From doing what you want…
Be… be in the moment…
Live in it with all your heart…
Immerse yourself in what(ever…) you are doing…
If at the moment you are still… not flowing…
Be in the stillness…
For it is conserving your energy before momentum…
Trust… Trust… Trust…
The process…
The purpose… will unfold…
There will be a day (and it will be…) sooner than you think…

Dealing with Endings

In life, if something starts, it is going to end sooner or later. Dealing with the ending is not an easy task for anyone as each one of us is attached to memories with experiences good or bad. We as humans know that everything which has its own form was once created and is going to end in the due course of time. It may even change form or its role.

We know this truth, yet we do not try to understand it. And then we get into unhealthy attachments, which creates resistance to let go. People get emotionally disturbed. They express this disturbance through various pessimistic responses. Blaming others or their situations are also a part of this emotional disturbance. While this emotional disturbance is a natural response and cannot be avoided, coming out of it is completely possible.

Not creating the emotional disturbance after an undesirable event is also possible. Considering the fact, acceptance of the situation is necessary. Acceptance gives one a whole new perspective to see the situation. It creates possibilities of new opportunities, of new beginnings. Every negative always has some positive. Surrendering, acceptance and forgiveness are keys to enhanced emotional states in case of endings, which leads to the opening of a new door, a new vision. And many times, a positive outcome.

Understanding Endings

If we see life as a chain series of events, each event changes into another and other into another and so on. In that case, there is no end, there is only change. Every end is a change of roles, responsibilities, appearances. It's like the law of energy. Energy is convertible, it cannot be created or destroyed, it changes form from one to another.

Anything that you consider yours is not yours in reality, you have simply come across it in your journey. Your role with that thing might change or remain constant, depending upon the Karma that you share. If your Karma is over, it will go away or change its form or role. There will be a creation of space where another thing will come and fit into. Hence dwelling in that void or crying over something that has already changed is a choice. At the same time, moving on to find something better than before or an improvement of yourself is another choice.

There is not a single person on earth who has not dealt with an ending. It's just 'how' one deals with it that changes the outcome. Every ending is not an ending in its actual form. If one takes it positively, wonders can happen. One may attract something that is far better. However, there should always be gratitude in our hearts for what lessons we have learnt from an ending. For every ending is a beginning... the beginning of a new experience, a new era.

Finding Yourself

Any kind of ending, whether it is losing your own self or finding your own self, is true, authentic. Once this process of finding yourself is complete, next comes the time to align yourself to this new version of yourself. Everyone often has a perspective of oneself that comes from the eyes of others. When you truly find yourself, the perspective of you that comes from others shatters, gets destroyed. It is tough for other people to accept this new version of you. For this, you need to accept yourself first. Accept the changes, the personality, the change in habit that has occurred. You have become a clean slate now. This acceptance of 'you' by 'you' is necessary.

After you accept yourself, the journey of the new 'you' begins. This journey comprises a few steps: initiation, determination, persuasion, and commitment.

Finding yourself, however, is not the end result. It is the beginning to go towards a new and better ending because everything that is created will end, or in other words, will change form. It's you who has changed your form for good. It's you who will grow tremendously from now on.

You grow...
When you stop underestimating yourself
When you stop people pleasing

When you no longer hide your true self
When you take pride in your being
When you no longer care what people will say
When you no longer need validation of others
When you feel complete within yourself
While playing the music of love....

Gratitude

There are about 8 billion human beings in the world at present, and the population is consistently increasing. Yet, we as humans do not meet everyone, we do not get to know everyone. We are born within a family, we make friends, some become acquaintances. Many that we were once close to go away from us, many unexpectedly become close. Why? Because we meet only those whom we were destined to meet.

We learn from everyone that we meet, whether they are or were good to us once, even those that weren't, those we could connect with or not. It's because they come into our lives to teach us something, to enrich our lives with some kind of experience. Therefore, whatever bond one shares with someone, one should always have gratitude for everyone they meet in their lives. This gratitude makes one more positive, more accepting as a person. Being grateful to every being and to the god, the creator can be the most fulfilling way of living.

Dear God
I see fragments of your essence everywhere
They are with me wherever I go
Whatever I do
There is a miniscule you
That peeps into my every decision

In my every doing
You judge me
Guide me, correct me
Tell me the difference
Between wrong and right
Whether you know it
Or not
In the process
Of this becoming
I am becoming you
Inch by inch
Breath by breath
Drop by drop
Day by day
In the mind and heart
I am carrying
The same shine
That shines through you

Whether you appreciate
Or not
Whether you acknowledge
Or not
You know deep within
That I too exist in you
For you are me
And I am you.